First Geography Encyclopedia

A DORLING KINDERSLEY BOOK

LONDON, NEW YORK,
MELBOURNE, MUNICH, and DELHI

Senior Editor Caroline Stamps
Written and edited by Wendy Horobin
and Caroline Stamps
Project Designer Gemma Fletcher
Design team Tory Gordon-Harris, Karen Hood,
Clare Marshall, Lauren Rosier, and Mary Sandberg

Consultant Clive Carpenter

Publishing Manager Bridget Giles
Art Director Martin Wilson
Category Publisher Mary Ling
Picture Researcher Harriet Mills
Production Editor Sean Daly
Production Controller Claire Pearson
Jacket Designer Gemma Fletcher
Jacket Editor Matilda Gollon

This edition published in 2013.
First published in Great Britain in 2010 by
Dorling Kindersley Limited,
80 Strand, London, WC2R 0RL

Penguin Group (UK)
10 9 8 7 6 5 4 3 2 1
001–178368–Jun/13

A CIP catalogue record for this book
is available from the British Library.

ISBN 978-1-4093-4151-2

Colour reproduction by MDP, UK
Printed and bound in China by
South China Printing Company Ltd.

Discover more at
www.dk.com

Contents

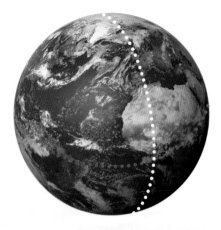

Introduction

Physical geography

There is a question at the bottom of each page...

The living world

Human geography

The wonderful world of maps

Reference section

About this book

The pages of this book have special features that will show you how to get your hands on as much information as possible! Look out for these:

The **Curiosity quiz** will get you searching through each section for the answers.

Become an expert tells you where to look for more information on a subject.

Every page is colour-coded to show you which section it is in.

Hands on Activities show you how you can try things out for yourself.

What is geography?

This is a book about geography. Geography is about the Earth and its people. Geography tells us about the world, the places where we live, and also how people's actions affect it.

Physical or human?

Geography can be divided into physical geography and human geography. These subjects are vast and cover lots of different areas of geography.

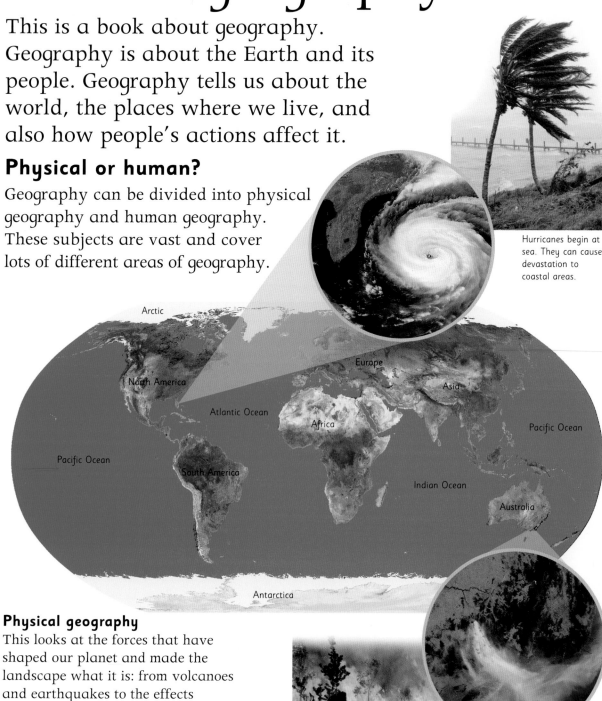

Hurricanes begin at sea. They can cause devastation to coastal areas.

Arctic

Europe

North America

Asia

Atlantic Ocean

Africa

Pacific Ocean

Pacific Ocean

South America

Indian Ocean

Australia

Antarctica

Physical geography

This looks at the forces that have shaped our planet and made the landscape what it is: from volcanoes and earthquakes to the effects of wind and rain.

Australia suffers from bushfires at certain times of the year.

Can you name an activity that affects how land is used?

Eratosthenes's map of the world was drawn more than 2,000 years ago.

Eratosthenes

Alexander von Humboldt (1769–1859)

The "father" of geography

Eratosthenes (276–194 BCE) was the first person to use the word "geography" in relation to the study of Earth. The word geography comes from ancient Greece, where "ge" meant "earth" and "grapho" meant "to write".

The founder of modern geography

German scientist Alexander von Humboldt travelled to the Americas and Europe, recording everything he observed about the landscapes he visited. His findings were published in a series of geography books.

Lots of work

All sorts of people work in the various fields of geography. Can you think of any?

 Cartographer Many types of maps are made by cartographers.

 Town planner New towns need careful planning.

 Ecologists study nature, but many link this to geographical features.

 Geologists look at the physical world – the rocks and minerals around us.

 Volcanologists study volcanic activity, hoping to predict eruptions.

Sheep herding in The Netherlands.

Human geography

Human activity also contributes to geography. Where we build, what we farm, our work, our travel, and even what we eat... all these things affect our planet.

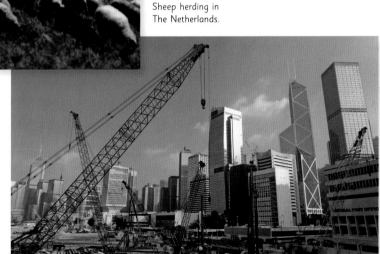

Construction site and skyline in Hong Kong.

Everything that people do involves using the land, from building to agriculture.

Our planet

Next time you go for a walk, take a look around you. Are there hills where you live? Are you near a river? Have you noticed how that river winds its way through the landscape? Welcome to the world of physical geography.

Physical what?

Physical geography is all about Earth – how it is formed, its mountains and rifts, its hills and valleys.

Mountains and lakes attract holidaymakers.

The water in Lake Grundlsee in Austria comes from melted snow and streams running off the mountains.

On which continent would you find Austria (where the picture above was taken)?

Cause and effect

The geography of an area – the natural surroundings – affects people's use of that area.

 Deserts People can and do live in particular desert areas, but life is hard.

 Rainforests Rich in plants and animals, rainforests today are under threat.

 Caves People have lived in caves in the past. Few people do so today.

 Islands Thousands of rocky islands are dotted around the world.

 Rivers These are a country's lifeblood. Many towns lie on river banks.

 Wetlands Water-soaked ground provides a natural and efficient water filter.

The lake is surrounded by mountains. This was once the site of a glacier.

Alpine forests thrive on lower mountain slopes.

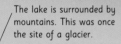

Curiosity quiz

Look through the Physical Geography pages and see if you can identify the picture clues below.

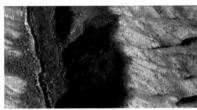

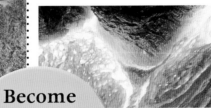

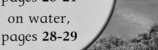

Become an expert...

on mountains, pages **20-21**

on water, pages **28-29**

A look at Earth

Earth is your home, but how much do you know about the blue and green planet that you live on? Below your feet, the ground isn't as solid as you think; Earth's outer layer, or crust, is only a very thin part of the whole planet and is broken into sections.

It is about 6,400 kilometres (4,000 miles) to the centre of the Earth.

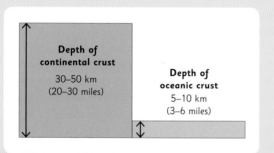

Depth of continental crust
30–50 km
(20–30 miles)

Depth of oceanic crust
5–10 km
(3–6 miles)

That's a thick bit!

We live on Earth's crust and so do an enormous variety of plants and animals. The crust's depth varies – it is thinner under the oceans than the continents.

Layered Earth

Earth is divided into four main layers: the crust, the mantle, and the outer and inner core. The inner core is thought to be a solid mass of iron and nickel. Iron is also one of the most common metals in Earth's crust and is mined from the Earth's crust to produce steel.

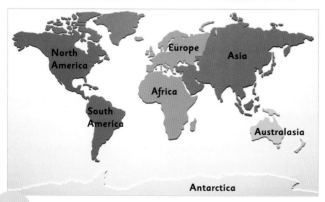

North America

Europe

Asia

Africa

South America

Australasia

Antarctica

What we see

Look at a world map and you will see large areas of land. These are known as continents. There are seven continents: Africa, Asia, North America, South America, Europe, Australasia (also called Oceania), and Antarctica.

How old is Earth?

A crust above
The outer layer of rock is called the crust.

Over millions of years, the hot rock in the mantle churns around like thick treacle, driven by heat from the core.

The outer core
Beneath the mantle, the outer core is made of liquid iron and nickel.

The inner core
The inner core is a solid ball of metal (iron and nickel). It is unbelievably hot.

The existence of a solid inner core was first suggested by Danish scientist Inge Lehmann in 1936.

Earth's mantle
The mantle sits below the crust. It is made of hot, almost solid rock.

Semi-solid rock slowly rises through the mantle, then cools and sinks back, to be heated once again.

Earth rocks

Our planet is made up of many different rocks and minerals.

 Granite is a typical land rock and is found in the crust. It is a hard rock.

 Basalt is also found in the crust, usually at the bottom of an ocean.

 Peridotite is the main rock found in Earth's upper mantle.

 Nickel is a magnetic metal that with iron makes up Earth's core.

Hidden heat

There is immense heat inside Earth. We know this because volcanoes occasionally erupt and lava (molten rock) bursts through the crust. This internal heat keeps the planet alive.

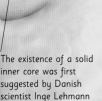
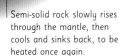

Earth is about four and a half billion years old.

On the move

Have you ever thought that the west coast of Africa and the east coast of South America look as if they could slot together? They once did! Two hundred million years ago, all the continents were joined as one enormous supercontinent, Pangaea.

Was there proof?

Support for Wegener was found in fossils of plants and animals that were discovered on different continents. Fossils of *Mesosaurus* (a reptile that lived 280 million years ago) were found on the Atlantic coasts of Africa and South America, indicating these lands were once joined.

Mesosaurus fossil

Moving continents

The idea that the continents move was suggested in 1915 by Alfred Wegener. He was convinced that the landmasses were once joined and had drifted apart.

270 million years ago a single supercontinent named Pangaea stood alone on a vast ocean.

200 million years ago
The continents had begun to appear, but North America was still connected to Europe.

TODAY This is the world as we know it, with its five huge oceans.

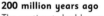
Scientists call the movement

So what's going on?

The ground beneath our feet is always on the move. That's because Earth's crust is made up of gigantic slabs of rock called plates, and these plates shift against each other.

10

Sliding around

Earth's plates move because they float on Earth's slow-moving mantle, which lies under its crust. The movement of Earth's plates means that the continents are shifting by anything from just 1 cm (½ in) to 10 cm (4 in) each year.

weird or what?

When Earth's plates move away from each other, the land above increases in size. Iceland is growing in this way – by just under 2.5 cm (1 inch) each year!

How do the plates move?

Earth's three types of plate move against each other in different ways:

Convergent plates move together. They cause mountain ranges to build.

Divergent plates move away from each other. It makes the land above grow in size.

Transform plates grind past each other. They cause earthquakes as they can suddenly slip.

On the edge

The areas where the plates meet are marked by high mountains, earthquake and volcanic zones, and deep ocean trenches.

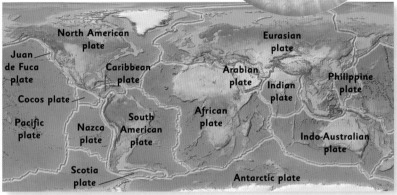

North American plate
Juan de Fuca plate
Caribbean plate
Cocos plate
Pacific plate
Nazca plate
South American plate
African plate
Arabian plate
Indian plate
Eurasian plate
Philippine plate
Indo-Australian plate
Scotia plate
Antarctic plate

The continents rest on huge slabs called tectonic plates.

Our understanding of Earth's plates is very new. A map showing Earth's plates first appeared in the 1960s.

Plates move slowly – but they move all the time.

of Earth's plates "tectonics".

Mount St Helens erupting in 1980

Mount St Helens is an active volcano in Washington, USA.

There are seven large plates and about twelve smaller ones.

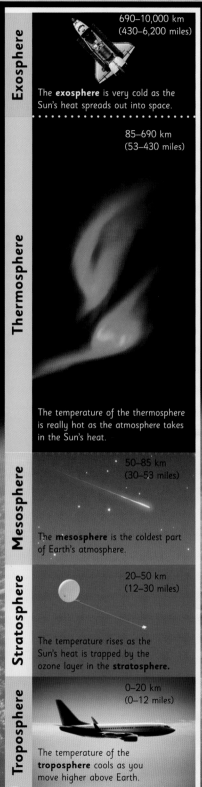

Exosphere

690–10,000 km
(430–6,200 miles)

The **exosphere** is very cold as the Sun's heat spreads out into space.

85–690 km
(53–430 miles)

Thermosphere

The temperature of the thermosphere is really hot as the atmosphere takes in the Sun's heat.

Mesosphere

50–85 km
(30–53 miles)

The **mesosphere** is the coldest part of Earth's atmosphere.

Stratosphere

20–50 km
(12–30 miles)

The temperature rises as the Sun's heat is trapped by the ozone layer in the **stratosphere.**

Troposphere

0–20 km
(0–12 miles)

The temperature of the **troposphere** cools as you move higher above Earth.

The atmosphere

Earth is wrapped in a thin blanket of gases known as our atmosphere. This protects us from the Sun's fierce power, and makes life on Earth possible.

Layer upon layer

The atmosphere is made up of a number of layers, divided according to temperature: the troposphere, the stratosphere, the mesosphere, the thermosphere, and the exosphere.

Most experts agree that outer space

Not so thick

Our atmosphere is thinner than you might think. If you could drive straight up in a car, it would take just 10 minutes to cross the troposphere, the first layer that contains all living things.

A helping hand

The oxygen in our atmosphere is produced by plants. That's why plants are vital to the survival of the planet: without them, we would run out of oxygen.

A plant's leaves release oxygen into the air.

Which layers make up the upper atmosphere?

What if there were no atmosphere?

The atmosphere traps some of the Sun's heat, which animals and plants need to survive. If there was no atmosphere, the Sun's rays would bounce off Earth and disappear into space.

Getting thinner

Earth's gravity holds the atmosphere in place. Most of the air we breathe and most of the moisture Earth produces is contained in the troposphere. This air thins the higher you are, resulting in less oxygen.

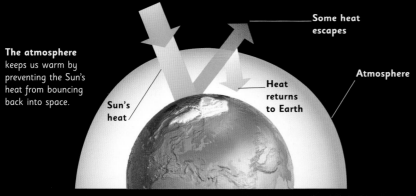

Some heat escapes

The atmosphere keeps us warm by preventing the Sun's heat from bouncing back into space.

Sun's heat

Heat returns to Earth

Atmosphere

Mountaineers need to carry a supply of oxygen to help them breathe.

starts at a height of 100 km (62 miles).

Protection from the Sun

One gas in the atmosphere protects Earth from harmful rays: ozone. An ozone hole above Antarctica created by chemical pollution is where the levels of ozone are lower than elsewhere.

Protection from bombardment

The atmosphere also helps to protect Earth from bombardment by meteors – space rocks. The Moon's surface is cratered because it has no atmosphere. Most meteors burn up as they fall through the atmosphere.

The ozone hole is the thinnest part of the ozone layer in the stratosphere. More of the Sun's harmful rays can get through here.

Meteors break up in the mesosphere. Some of the large pieces that are not burned up make craters when they hit Earth.

Rocky planet

Our planet is a ball of molten and solid rock. You see Earth's rocks in mountains and by rivers. People called geologists study rocks, because they can tell us a lot about our planet.

Are rocks permanent?

No! Rocks are constantly eroded – they are broken down by wind and rain, or ice and snow. There is a rock cycle, which sees continuous shifting between the different types of rock over millions of years.

The rock cycle

There are three main types of rock, all caught in a continuous (but long) rock cycle.

Igneous rocks form when hot, molten rock (magma) cools and turns solid.

can form

can form

can form

can form

can form

Metamorphic rocks are heated and squashed deep under Earth's surface.

Sedimentary rocks are made from layers of sand, mud, or sea creatures.

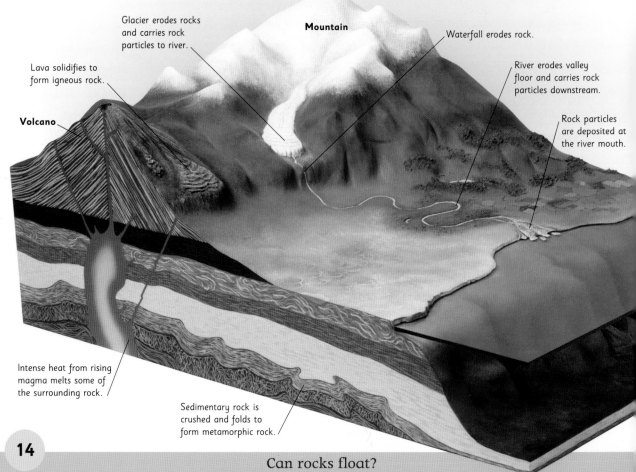

Glacier erodes rocks and carries rock particles to river.

Mountain

Waterfall erodes rock.

Lava solidifies to form igneous rock.

River erodes valley floor and carries rock particles downstream.

Volcano

Rock particles are deposited at the river mouth.

Intense heat from rising magma melts some of the surrounding rock.

Sedimentary rock is crushed and folds to form metamorphic rock.

Can rocks float?

Minerals

Rocks are made up from substances called minerals. Most rocks are mixtures of two or more minerals. That's why there are lots of different coloured rocks. Gold and silver are minerals, as is diamond.

Feldspar (pink and white) Mica (black)

Quartz (grey)

Quartz crystals + **Feldspar crystals** + **Mica crystals** = **Granite (a type of rock)**

This spiral-shaped fossil is the lower jaw of a **Helicoprion** shark.

This fossil was found in limestone.

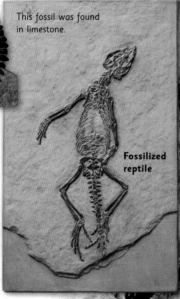

Fossilized reptile

Layers of sediment can be clearly seen on this cliff face.

Fossil finds

The fact that rocks haven't always been solid is shown by the presence of fossils. These are the impressions of long-dead plants and animals. When they died, their bodies fell into swamps or marshes, which squashed down over them.

Lighter rock particles collect on the ocean floor and form layers of sediment.

Layers of sediment are squashed together and gradually harden to form sedimentary rock.

We use them!

Rocks and minerals are mined to provide many of the things we use every day, from materials for our buildings to computers and jewellery.

Pumice stone is an igneous volcanic rock that floats.

Exploding Earth

An erupting volcano has the power to change the landscape around it, and in ways you may not expect. Flowing lava is dangerous, but did you know that a volcano can also affect the weather?

What is a volcano?

A volcano is an opening in Earth's crust. Most volcanoes lie above spots where the different plates of Earth's crust meet.

Red fire spots mark some of Earth's active volcanoes.

Not all volcanoes lie on plate boundaries.

Volcanic islands dot the Pacific.

Red lines mark the places where Earth's plates meet.

Why does it happen?

Volcanoes erupt if the molten rock beneath them, called magma, builds up to such an intense pressure that it needs to be released. It can burst out with explosive force.

Red-hot river

Everything in the path of a lava flow will be destroyed. The shifts happening beneath the surface can also cause earthquakes.

A flow of lava will set fire to anything caught in its path.

What is molten rock (magma) called once it erupts out of a volcano?

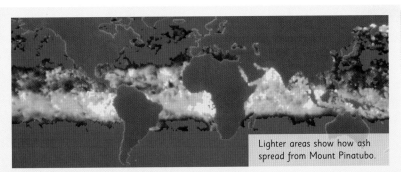

Lighter areas show how ash spread from Mount Pinatubo.

How can a volcano affect weather?

Dust and ash can rain down for days after an eruption, entering the atmosphere and affecting our weather by blocking sunlight. The 1991 eruption of Mount Pinatubo lowered world temperatures by 0.5°C (1°F) for a year! Dense ash clouds can also stop aircraft flights.

Not all the same!

Three types of lava are produced by a volcano.

Aa lava moves quickly and it hardens to form sharp chunks.

Pahoehoe lava moves slowly. Usually it forms smooth, rope-shaped rock.

Pillow lava produces large blobs. It usually forms under water.

Eruptions often result in lightning. It's caused by fragments of lava in the ash cloud rubbing together so much it creates an electrical charge.

This extinct volcano in Madagascar has been covered with crop fields.

Too hot to walk on?

Lava forms a crust hard enough to step on after about 15 minutes, but it can remain hot beneath for several hours or even days, depending on how thick it is.

New growth

Although a volcano causes devastation, the ash that settles provides a healthy fertilizer for new growth, and the plants that return will grow quickly. It can provide a rich base for farmland.

It is called lava.

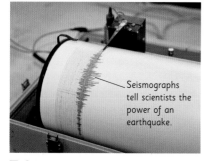

Seismographs tell scientists the power of an earthquake.

Taking a measurement

Earthquakes are recorded on seismographs, a machine that produces a wiggly line. The larger the wiggle, the more powerful the earthquake.

Earthquake!

There have already been several earthquakes today. Earthquakes happen every day. Most are mild, or so far from cities that they go undetected apart from being picked up on special equipment. Some are more serious.

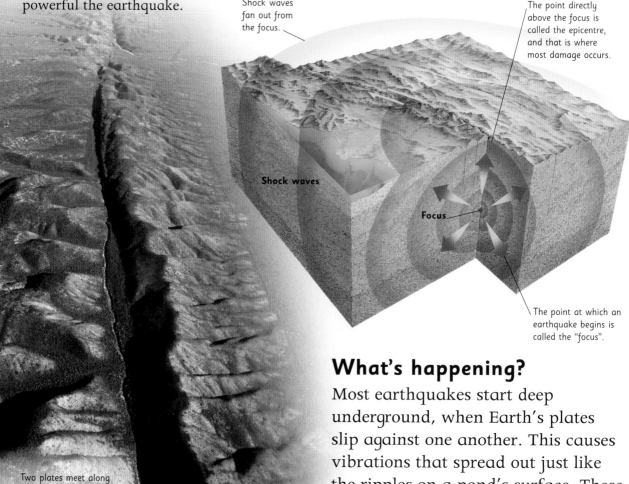

Shock waves fan out from the focus.

The point directly above the focus is called the epicentre, and that is where most damage occurs.

Shock waves

Focus

The point at which an earthquake begins is called the "focus".

Two plates meet along the San Andreas Fault, which runs through California, USA.

What's happening?

Most earthquakes start deep underground, when Earth's plates slip against one another. This causes vibrations that spread out just like the ripples on a pond's surface. These shock waves shake the surrounding rock and soil as they pass through.

What is the study of earthquakes called?

Growth of a tsunami

Sometimes, a major earthquake will trigger a tsunami, a gigantic wave that can cause devastation if it hits land.

The tsunami may cause floods that can damage coastal areas.

The water is at first drawn back by the powerful suction from the tsunami.

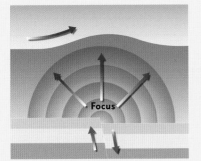

Deep beneath the ocean's floor, an earthquake sends out shock waves.

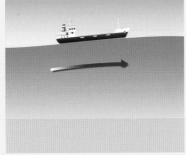

The shock wave causes a surge of water to travel across the ocean.

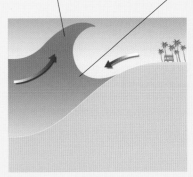

When the surge of water reaches a coastline, it becomes a tsunami.

A destructive force

An earthquake's shock waves may be strong enough to shake buildings and even cause them to fall. Many buildings in cities vulnerable to earthquakes are built following strict building controls.

A fiery ring

More then 70 per cent of all earthquakes occur on spots in a ring around the Pacific Ocean. Known as the "ring of fire", this line marks the edge of the huge Pacific Plate where it meets other plates.

Not all buildings are built to withstand an earthquake.

Making mountains

Twenty per cent of Earth's land surface is mountainous. How are these steep-sided rock masses born?

The Himalayas include Mt Everest, the world's highest mountain.

Survival

Many plants and animals have adapted to survive mountain life.

Conifers are evergreen trees that have thick, waxy leaves.

Andean condors soar high about the mountain peaks of South America.

Snow leopards from central Asia have thick fur and bushy tails.

People! About 10 per cent of the world's population live in mountain regions.

Not just any old mountain!

Mountains form over the course of millions of years because of the movements of Earth's plates pushing against each other. They are not all the same; there are fold, block, dome, and volcanic mountains.

Peaks of the Patagonian Andes

Mountain peaks are often shrouded in clouds and have weather that can change in the blink of an eye.

Why are mountain tops so jagged?

That's because they are constantly eroded by the weather, which wears the rocky surface away. Over millions of years, a mountain will crumble!

Are there mountains beneath the oceans?

Fold mountains

... are the most common of all mountains. They develop when Earth's plates collide, lifting Earth's crust and pushing it over on itself. The Himalayas are fold mountains, and they are still rising – but only by about 1 metre (3¼ ft) every 1,000 years.

1. A simple diagram shows how fold mountains form. First, layers of sediments are laid down.

2. Z-shaped folds begin to appear as one of Earth's plates pushes into a neighbouring plate.

3. As the plate continues to push, more folds are created in the ground above.

4. After millions of years, movements of the plates have resulted in a series of mountains.

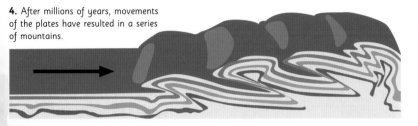

What is a mountain range?

Mountains tend to occur in groups, called ranges. The longest range on land is the Andes, which stretches for 7,200 km (4,470 miles) down the western edge of South America.

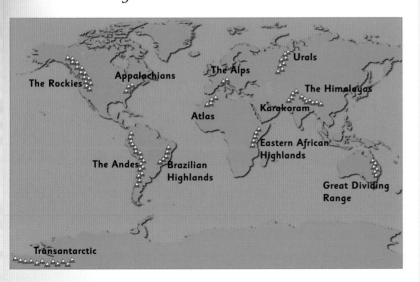

The Rockies · Appalachians · The Alps · Urals · The Himalayas · Karakoram · Atlas · Eastern African Highlands · The Andes · Brazilian Highlands · Great Dividing Range · Transantarctic

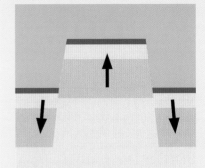

Block mountains
These begin to form when a slab of land breaks off and is forced up as two of Earth's plates pull apart or push together. Germany's Harz Mountains are block mountains.

Volcanic mountains
The Hawaiian islands are volcanic mountains. They formed from layers of cooled and hardened lava and ash after a series of long volcanic eruptions.

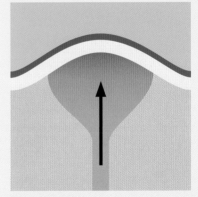

Dome mountains
These occur when molten rock forces the ground above it upwards, but it doesn't break through the surface. The force, or pressure, produces a dome-like shape.

Yes. The world's largest mountain ranges are covered by the oceans.

A look at islands

An island is a piece of land surrounded by water. There are thousands, of all different sizes, formed in different ways: some by earthquake, some by erosion, and some by volcanic action.

An island's sandy shores provide clues as to how the island formed.

Clues in the sand

If an island has black sand, it formed from volcanic ash. If the sand is white, it formed from ground coral.

A chain of islands

Some places are made up of islands, dotted around the ocean like jewels on a necklace. Indonesia is one such place. It is made up of more than 13,700 islands, scattered over a huge area.

Indonesia's islands span 5,000 km (3,100 miles) – or one-eighth of Earth's circumference!

This St Lawrence island has become a private estate.

Nothing's too small

The "Thousand Islands" are found in the St Lawrence River between the USA and Canada. There are actually about 1,800 of them, including many tiny ones, some of which have been built on.

Name the "island continent".

River islands

Islands can form at the mouth of a river, where it meets the ocean. This is due to the river water dumping sediment in shallow water. The river flows around it, and an island – or islands – begins to form.

This island has formed at the mouth of a river where sediment has built up.

The Galápagos Islands consist of about 15 main islands. This satellite image shows three of them.

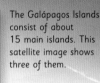

I'm pretty special!

Islands are often home to unique plants and animals. One example is the marine iguana, the world's only lizard to live in the sea and eat seaweed. It is found only on the Galápagos Islands.

Marine iguana

I see new islands!

Ring-shaped coral reef islands (atolls) form when corals grow in shallow water around an ocean volcano. Over time, the volcano cone erodes, leaving a ring of coral, which leads to the formation of sandy islands.

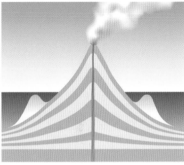

A volcano is born in a tropical sea, building up a huge cone. Corals begin to move in around the volcano.

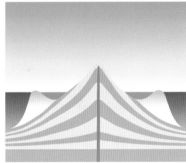

Wave and wind action erode the volcano's cone over thousands of years. However, the ring of coral is thriving.

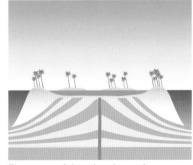

The erosion of the volcano's cone leaves a submerged crater. Sand is swept onto the coral, resulting in small islands.

Australia.

Birth of an island

If a volcano erupts under the sea, it can pour out enough rock to form a new island in a matter of days. One such island is Surtsey, which appeared off the coast of Iceland in 1963.

Surtsey is a tiny island off the south coast of Iceland.

How long to make an island?

Not as long as you might think! Surtsey was formed between 1963 and June 1967, when the volcano beneath finally stopped erupting. Surtsey is now home to a variety of animals and plants.

The birth of Surtsey in 1963 was witnessed by fishermen, who saw a huge plume of smoke erupting from violent explosions in the water.

By 1967, Surtsey was an island, and the volcano had stopped its constant eruptions. It measured 2.7 square km (1 square mile).

A special place

Botanists and biologists have learnt much by studying the arrival and survival of life on Surtsey. There is a research station there, but few people are allowed to visit the island.

Has Surtsey continued to grow?

Birds arrive

In 1970, the first sea birds began to settle on Surtsey, building their nests on the cliffs. The first to arrive included Northern fulmars and black guillemots as well as great black-backed gulls. Puffins have also been spotted on Surtsey.

Northern fulmar

Become an expert...
on volcanoes, pages **16-17**
on islands, pages **22-23**

How life arrived

It is amazing how fast life reaches an island, and in different ways.

Seeds are brought by passing birds, or may be carried on the wind.

Floating tufts of grass provide mini rafts for insects and seeds.

Spiders are thought to have drifted to Surtsey on the wind.

Birds find the island provides a useful resting place.

Seals, too!

Common seals sought out the sheltered coves of Surtsey and were joined in 1982 by grey seals.

Common seal

Plants take root

Volcanic ash provides a rich soil for plants, and they were quick to appear on Surtsey, including a number of flowering plants as well as mosses. Most people would recognize two of the plants on Surtsey: the common dandelion and the buttercup.

Dandelion

Buttercup

No. Since the volcano stopped, the island has shrunk owing to erosion.

Under attack

When you go for a walk in the countryside or by the coast, the landscape around you looks permanent, but it's not. Mountains, hills, the coastline – all are under attack from a process called erosion.

Attack by wind and rain

Hoodoos, or earth pyramids, are columns of sandstone capped by harder rock. Repeated pummelling by wind and rain wear away at the softer sandstone, leaving spectacular shapes.

Attack by ice
Rock fragments (scree) on a mountain's slopes are usually the result of ice forming in cracks and splitting the rock. Scree sometimes lands on roads cut through mountains.

These hoodoos in Turkey were once hollowed into homes.

What happens when erosion occurs?

Attack by running water

Rivers carve the easiest path through a landscape, and make huge changes to its appearance. Over millions of years, the Colorado River has carved America's mighty Grand Canyon, which at its deepest is now 1,829 m (6,000 ft).

The Colorado River has carved its way through layer after layer of soft limestone.

Attack by land

Occasionally a mass of loose soil and rocks will slip down a hill in a landslide that engulfs everything in its path. Landslides usually occur after heavy rain or snow.

Attack by the sea

Rocky coastlines suffer constant battering by the sea. Sea stacks are an obvious example of how parts of the coast can become separated from the mainland, as softer rock falls away to leave them standing alone.

How do stacks form?

Sea stacks are formed by coastal erosion.

Waves driven by high winds repeatedly batter the cliff.

The continued battering causes the cliff to erode at its base, forming an arch.

The top of the arch collapses, leaving a stack. A second arch has now formed.

The Twelve Apostles are sea stacks that stand off the coast of Victoria, Australia.

A large object is broken down into smaller pieces.

Water works

Viewed from above the Pacific Ocean, Earth appears to be almost completely covered in water.

Water is all around us, as well as inside us. It is in the air as water vapour, it fills the world's oceans and rivers, and it soaks into the ground. There would be no life without water.

Salty water

Most of Earth's water is salty. Sea water has a high salt content because the water has picked up minerals on its journey to the sea.

Reservoir near Marseille, France

Journey to the tap
Huge reservoirs collect and store fresh water. Cleaned water is sent along pipes to supply people's homes and offices. Not everyone has access to clean water.

Water evaporation

Water evaporates from the oceans. That means it changes into a gas and rises as water vapour.

Mountain tops have a permanent covering of ice and snow.

Frozen water
About 80 per cent of Earth's fresh water is frozen. It makes up the polar ice caps, and forms glaciers. It also caps the tops of mountains.

Salt deposits on rocks on the shores of the Dead Sea.

Can you name another form of precipitation?

Going around and around

The Sun's heat causes a constant water cycle, where water moves from land to ocean, and up into the atmosphere... again and again.

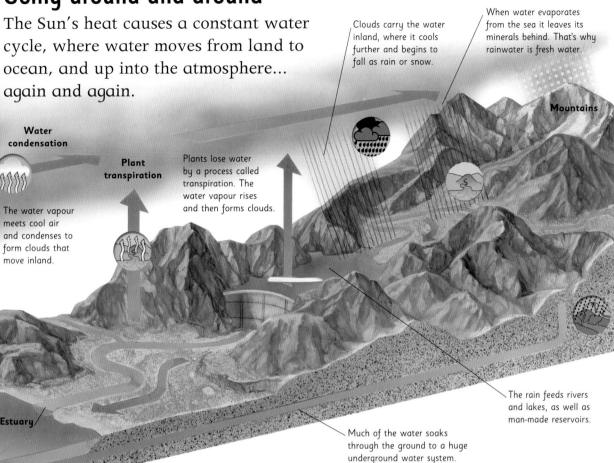

Clouds carry the water inland, where it cools further and begins to fall as rain or snow.

When water evaporates from the sea it leaves its minerals behind. That's why rainwater is fresh water.

Mountains

Water condensation

The water vapour meets cool air and condenses to form clouds that move inland.

Plant transpiration

Plants lose water by a process called transpiration. The water vapour rises and then forms clouds.

Estuary

The rain feeds rivers and lakes, as well as man-made reservoirs.

Much of the water soaks through the ground to a huge underground water system.

It's all here!

The water cycle is made up of six key parts, or processes. These are shown on the diagram above.

 Evaporation is when a liquid changes into a gas. Water from the oceans heats up and rises as vapour.

 Condensation happens when a gas changes into a liquid. When water vapour cools it forms clouds.

 Precipitation means water is falling to Earth as snow, rain, or hail.

 Infiltration is when rainwater soaks into the ground. Its speed depends on how porous the soil is.

 Runoff happens as rainwater flows downhill and into streams, rivers, ponds, and lakes.

 Transpiration is when water evaporates from plant leaves and enters the air as water vapour.

Fresh water

Fresh water comprises just three per cent of the total water on Earth, but most of it is hidden from view, deep under the ground.

Rivers

A river forms after fresh water runs downhill from a hill or mountain source, twisting and turning and collecting more water from streams (called tributaries) as it heads towards the ocean. On the way, it shapes the landscape and is used as a valuable resource.

The meeting of two differently coloured rivers makes a striking contrast in Montana, USA.

Missouri River

The Missouri is nicknamed "Big Muddy".

The Milk River

A frozen river

Glaciers are "rivers" of ice and rock found in polar mountain regions. They move downhill slowly, carving out deep U-shaped valleys and picking up huge boulders.

Why are rivers different colours?

A river's colour depends on the land it runs through. The Milk River is named for its pale colour, created by the sediment it picks up. The colour difference is stark when it meets the Missouri, in Montana.

The power of water

Rivers and streams wear away rock and carry this material, called sediment, over a vast distance. This stream has damaged a road in Washington State, USA.

Does the River Nile just flow through one country?

The world's longest rivers

Rivers are hard to measure, because some measurements take in streams, or combine rivers, while others don't. These are the longest rivers in six of the world's seven continents.

VOLGA 3,530 km (2,190 miles) Europe's longest river.

MURRAY-DARLING 3,750 km (2,330 miles) Australasia's longest river.

MISSISSIPPI-MISSOURI 6,020 km (3,740 miles) North America's longest river.

YANGTZE (CHANG JIANG) 6,300 km (3,915 miles) Asia's longest river.

AMAZON 6,450 km (4,005 miles) South America's longest river.

NILE 6,670 km (4,145 miles) Africa's longest river.

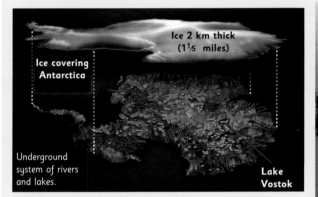

Ice 2 km thick (1⅕ miles)

Ice covering Antarctica

Underground system of rivers and lakes.

Lake Vostok

A flood may mean people have to be evacuated as happened during this flood in California, USA.

What about Antarctica?

Antarctic rivers are small – the River Onyx is just 40 km (25 miles) in length, and despite its name is actually a stream. However, scientists believe that deep under Antarctica there are many rivers and lakes.

All sorts of uses

Among other things, rivers supply us with:

Recreation From rowing boats to windsurfing, rivers can be used for fun.

Food People have fished in rivers for thousands of years.

Transportation Rivers connect cities and towns with the coast.

Energy The flow of rivers has long been used to drive machinery.

Farming River water is used by farmers throughout the world.

We've been flooded

Many rivers burst their banks, bringing devastation to local communities. It can happen after a heavy downpour of rain or following a long period of wet weather.

No. It flows through Burundi, Uganda, Ethiopia, Sudan, and Egypt.

Caves

From limestone caverns to lava tubes, enter a cave and you walk into a dark, and often damp, world. It is a world of spectacular structures and peculiar shapes.

It may take 100 years for a stalactite to grow just 1 cm (½ inch).

Stalagmites usually grow up below a stalactite. If the two join, they form a column.

Cave wildlife

Caves have sheltered animals – and humans – for centuries.

Bats Many bats roost in caves, hooking their claws into the ceiling.

Blind Texas salamander This rare amphibian makes its home in Texas, USA.

Blind cave fish This cave-dwelling fish was first found in China in 1997.

European cave spider As an adult this spider cannot bear light.

Olm This European amphibian has excellent smell and hearing.

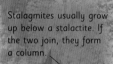
weird or what?
Lava tubes are volcanic tunnel caves created when red-hot lava pushes through a hardened outer layer. They can be long. Australia's Undara lava tube runs for 100 kilometres (62 miles)!

Slow growth

Limestone cave systems often contain amazing structures. These are formed as dripping water leaves stony deposits that grow down from the ceiling (stalactites) or build upwards from the cave floor (stalagmites).

What are troglodytes?

Water seeps into the ground, wearing away the rock.

How a cave forms

All because of water

Limestone caves are created over thousands of years by water steadily wearing away at rock — the water's action carries away soft limestone rock, leaving the harder surrounding rock.

Coastal cave

Caves are sometimes created by the constant pounding of waves on exposed coastal rock. The pounding wears away at cracks in the rock face, forcing gaps that slowly enlarge into caves.

Some Yucatán rivers are open to the sky, forming natural wells called cenotes.

Going underground

Most of the world's fresh water is underneath the ground. In Yucatán, Mexico, there is little surface water — but there are plenty of underground rivers.

The world's mightiest crystals

The Crystal Caves of Mexico (*Cueva de los Cristales*) were only discovered in 2000. The main cavern contains huge crystals. The cave is hot and humid — temperatures reach 58°C (136°F).

People have to carry breathing equipment and wear protective clothing in the crystal caves.

Troglodytes are people who live in caves.

Climate

Climate is not the same as weather. An area's climate is the average weather for that area over time. A rainforest is hot and damp, while the poles suffer freezing temperatures.

KEY:

Dry

Tropical

Temperate

Subtropical

Cold

Weather can change

Tropic of Cancer

Equator

Regions further away from the equator receive less of the Sun's heat.

Climate looks

Two different climates:

The Philippines have a hot and damp tropical climate.

Italy has a subtropical climate.

World climates

Each of the world's regions has a particular climate. A world climate map shows how these regions fall into five loose bands across the world.

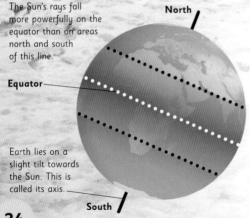

The Sun's rays fall more powerfully on the equator than on areas north and south of this line.

North

Equator

Earth lies on a slight tilt towards the Sun. This is called its axis.

South

What affects climate?

Climate depends on an area's distance from the equator and from the coast, and its height above sea level. Locations near to the equator feel more of the heat from the Sun because of Earth's tilt on its axis.

How many different climates are experienced in Australia?

It's cooler – there are mountains!

Features in the surrounding landscape can also change an area's climate.

in minutes.

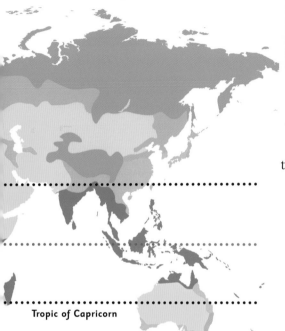

Tropic of Capricorn

Mountain ranges bring cooler weather to an area.

It's warmer here!

When a small area has a different climate to that of its surroundings, it's said to have a microclimate. It often happens in a city centre, where the air temperature can be a little higher than the countryside around it because buildings and roads hold the Sun's heat longer than trees and grass.

at weather conditions over time.

Temperatures in a large city may be a few degrees higher than the surrounding area.

Climate and clothes

A country's climate affects how its people dress, their houses, and the crops they grow. Flat-roofed houses are common in areas with little rain, while pitched roofs are seen in rainy areas.

Become an expert...

on weather, pages 36-37
on climate change, pages 38-39

These children are in warm clothing to protect them from the chilly climate of Siberia.

Four: Dry, tropical, subtropical, and temperate.

Weather

"It's windy!" "It's pouring with rain." "It's sunny – let's go out and play." The weather often affects what we do, but how does it happen? What brings changes in the weather?

How weather happens

All weather occurs in the lower layer of Earth's atmosphere. It happens because the Sun's heat warms the air here to different levels in different places. That makes the air move, causing winds... and winds bring changes in the weather.

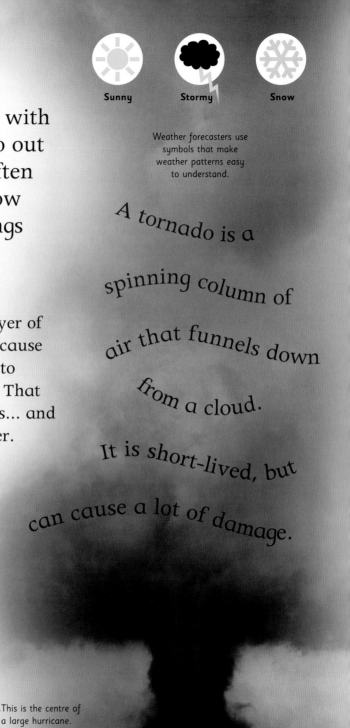

Sunny   Stormy   Snow

Weather forecasters use symbols that make weather patterns easy to understand.

A tornado is a spinning column of air that funnels down from a cloud. It is short-lived, but can cause a lot of damage.

This is the centre of a large hurricane.

Hurricanes build up over the ocean and move towards land, where they begin to lose power.

How can a pine cone be used to forecast the weather?

What are clouds?

Clouds are collections of moisture and are made up of ice crystals or water droplets. These are so tiny that they float. If too much moisture builds up, the droplets become too heavy to float on the air and fall to Earth as rain or snow or hail.

Thunderstorms can result in lightning striking the ground.

Hands on

Make a rain gauge. Tape a ruler to the side of a jar and add a funnel. Leave outside and record the rainfall each day. Empty and compare a second week.

There's a rainbow!

If sunlight breaks through on a rainy day, you may see a rainbow, as the Sun's rays pass through water.

What's happening?

From clear blue skies to wind and snow, all sorts of things can happen with our weather.

Winds may bring storms or rain. They can be light, or move at hurricane force.

Rain occurs when moisture in the air builds up in clouds.

Snow falls after water vapour changes to ice crystals inside a cloud.

Thunderstorms bring thunder and lightning and huge black clouds.

Waterspouts are tornadoes that happen over water. They form spinning columns of water.

Fog is formed from cloud at ground level. The air is full of moisture and feels damp and chilly.

What's the weather today?

A weather forecast tells us what is going to happen over the next few days. It helps people to plan – that's important for people such as pilots and farmers.

Weather balloon Special balloons carry equipment into the atmosphere to measure air temperature and pressure. The balloon pops and the equipment is returned safely to Earth by parachute.

Hurricane plane This aeroplane is equipped to study wind patterns around hurricanes.

Stevenson screen This protects equipment that collects information about the weather.

Satellite High above us, weather satellites help to predict what the weather will do.

A pine cone's scales will close up if wet weather is on the way.

Climate change

Our planet has gone through many changes of climate in its long history. Increasing temperatures show that Earth is getting hotter, but this time, human activity may be responsible.

Environmental change
Climate change may have a huge impact on the environment. Wetlands may dry up, or mountains receive more snow, making it harder for the species that live there to survive.

Most greenhouse gases come from the burning of fuel by power stations, aeroplanes, and cars.

Burping cows are a major source of methane

If there is too much carbon dioxide in the atmosphere it will trap the heat around Earth like a giant duvet.

The atmosphere
Earth's atmosphere keeps our planet warm. It contains gases such as carbon dioxide, water vapour, and methane, which prevent heat from leaking out into space. But if the levels of these gases increase, Earth could turn into a giant greenhouse.

Clean technologies can reduce the amount of pollutants and gases entering the atmosphere.

How many litres of methane can a cow produce every day?

Wild weather

Rising temperatures could also affect our weather. Countries in North Africa may become hotter and drier, while northern Europe could turn colder and wetter. Hurricanes and typhoons would increase and cause severe flooding. Other parts of the planet would suffer long droughts.

Costa Rican golden toad

Wildlife in peril

If animals and plants are unable to move to a new place or adapt to the new conditions, then they could die out. This has already happened to the Costa Rican golden toad.

If climate change happens some areas will get more extreme weather events.

Hands on
We can all do our bit by helping to save energy. You can do this by switching off lights and electrical equipment after use, turning down the heating, and walking to school.

What will happen?

No one is sure, but the effects could be drastic. The ice in glaciers and at the poles could melt and sea levels would rise. This would flood low-lying areas, such as Bangladesh, and coral islands in the Pacific Ocean.

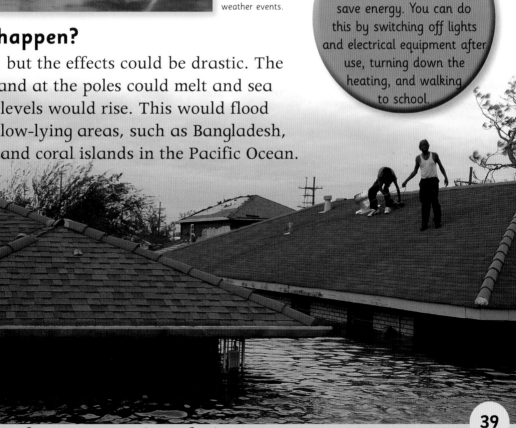

Around 200 litres (53 gallons). That's a lot of gas!

Looking after our Earth

Every day, we damage our planet. We cut down trees, dig up minerals, and pollute our soil and water. But there is a lot we can do to take care of our Earth.

What's the problem?

Cutting down trees

People use wood for many things: building houses, making paper, or burning as fuel.

Cutting trees increases soil erosion.

But we have cut down many of the forests that used to cover Earth. This is affecting the balance of gases in the atmosphere.

What to do: It's important that we plant new trees to replace the ones we cut down. In many countries forests are planted especially for harvesting. When they are cut they are replaced with new young trees.

A managed forest

Damaging land

Humans have been changing the landscape for centuries through farming, mining, and

Building replaces soil with concrete.

building. In some places this has led to erosion of the soil, landslides, and loss of homes for many species.

What to do: Damaged land can be restored in various ways. Careful use of fertilizer and growing plants to anchor the soil can halt erosion. Locally, small areas of waste ground can be turned into gardens or parks.

Planting urban gardens can make up for land clearance.

What things from your house can be recycled?

This power station has planted trees nearby to absorb (take in) pollutants.

Use and replace

One way to look after our planet is to make sure that everything we take from it is replaced or used carefully. That way we can protect our environment and keep it healthy and safe for every species on Earth. We call this sustainable development.

What you can do to help:

Don't drop litter in the street – pick it up and put it in a bin.

Plant things – even a window box of flowers or vegetables can help.

Switch off lights and electrical equipment after use to save energy.

Recycle as much as you can. Most household items can be reused.

Poisonous pollution

We need industry to provide many of the things we use in daily life, but it has a cost.

Oil spills can damage a wide area.

Pouring smoke into the atmosphere, or dumping waste on land or into waterways harms people, animals, and plants.

What to do: Most countries have laws that prevent companies from polluting the environment. This can also help industries to develop less wasteful ways of processing materials or find new uses for waste products.

Getting around

Every year, there are more and more cars on our planet, but the more journeys we make,

Traffic jams waste fuel.

the more land we have to destroy to make roads, and the more petrol fumes will poison the air.

What to do: If you're not going far, try to walk or ride a bicycle instead of going by car. And for longer journeys, why not use public transport, such as the bus or train?

Pedal power is environmentally friendly – and it keeps you fit!

Cleaning up oil pollution is hard work.

Paper, glass, metal, plastic, and fabrics.

The living world

When you look at all the different types of places that exist on Earth, it is hard not to be amazed by the huge variety of things that live there.

Beetle

Owl

Life

Living things, whether plant or animal, share certain characteristics. They all need food, and most need oxygen.

Animals

The animal kingdom is made up of animals with a backbone (vertebrates) and animals without a backbone (invertebrates). Animals have to move around to find food.

Buttercup

Ladybird

Plants

Plants use the Sun's energy to make their food. This is because unlike most animals, they cannot move to find food.

Tiger

Snail

Name an animal that cannot move.

Fungi

Toadstools and mushrooms are neither plants nor animals. They are fungi. Fungi absorb the nutrients they need from living or dead animals or plants.

Many fungi, like these, are poisonous to eat.

Alfalfa, a crop used to feed cattle, is being grown in a desert area.

Our environment

People can control their environment, but there is often a cost. These huge desert crop circles are 1 km (½ mile) in diameter. However, to grow the crop successfully requires vast quantities of water.

SLOW DOWN

PENGUINS CROSSING

A helping hand

The natural world can be destroyed by the effects of deforestation, farming, or building. People sometimes look for ways of helping animals under threat. Animal tunnels are built under roads, while signs are used to warn road users of animal crossing sites.

Curiosity quiz

Look through the Living World pages and see if you can identify the picture clues below.

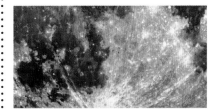

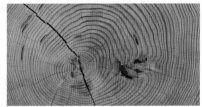

Become an expert...

on biomes, pages 46-47
on ecosystems, pages 48-49

The Goldilocks planet

Earth is known as the "Goldilocks" planet, because it is perfect for life. It is neither too hot nor too cold. Why? It's partly because our planet is neither too near to its star (our Sun) nor too far away. It is just right.

Our Sun

Thanks to its size, the Sun is about half way through its lifespan of nine billion years. That's long enough for life to become well established. If our Sun were larger, it would burn out more quickly, while a smaller Sun wouldn't be stable enough.

Seen from space, the atmosphere appears as a thin blue layer that encircles our planet.

Our Earth

None of the other planets in our solar system could support life as we know it. Earth's size means its gravity is just right to hold on to its atmosphere. That atmosphere not only protects us from the Sun's harmful rays, it also traps the Sun's heat, keeping us at the right temperature.

Where did the term "Goldilocks planet" originate?

The Sun

Mercury

Venus

Jupiter

Mars

Saturn

Neptune

Uranus

Earth

Water

We need water to survive. Our bodies contain a lot of water, and we need to drink water to keep our bodies working properly. Earth has plenty of water and, most importantly, it is on the planet's surface in liquid form.

Liquid water

Earth is the only planet in the solar system that lies the right distance from the Sun so that water remains liquid on its surface. Of the planets next to us, Mars is too far from the Sun, so it is too cold. Venus is too close and far too hot.

Less than one per cent of Earth's fresh water is to be found in rivers and lakes. Most water is saltwater and is found in the oceans.

Our Moon

The Moon helps to keep Earth's rotation stable and without it, there would be huge changes in the weather. It also affects the ocean's tides, and many believe that this was important in the development of life from the sea – leaving a coastal area that was covered by water and then exposed.

A giant's protection

Jupiter plays a major part in helping our planet. Jupiter's size means its gravity is stronger than Earth's, so it pulls lots of space rubble towards it. As a result, it protects us from impacts from asteroids and passing comets.

45

We live here!

The world can be divided into different types of landscape. These zones support different types of plants and animals, and are known as "biomes". Let's take a look at some biomes.

Coniferous forests
Evergreen conifers have adapted to survive in areas of long, cold winters and short summers.

Deserts
This is the driest of all biomes. Deserts can be hot or cold. Very little survives in a desert.

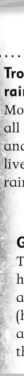

Tropical rainforests
More than half of all Earth's plant and animal species live in tropical rainforests.

Grasslands
These areas support huge numbers of animals that graze (herbivores) and the animals that hunt them (carnivores).

What are the other names for grasslands?

Polar regions

The areas surrounding the Arctic and Antarctic may be freezing but they support a wide variety of life.

Polar bears are found in the Arctic.

Tundra

Areas of tundra border the Arctic. This is a harsh biome, where the lower layers of soil are frozen, and plants are small and sparse. Few trees survive in tundra.

Temperate forests

Trees growing in temperate forests lose their leaves in the autumn.

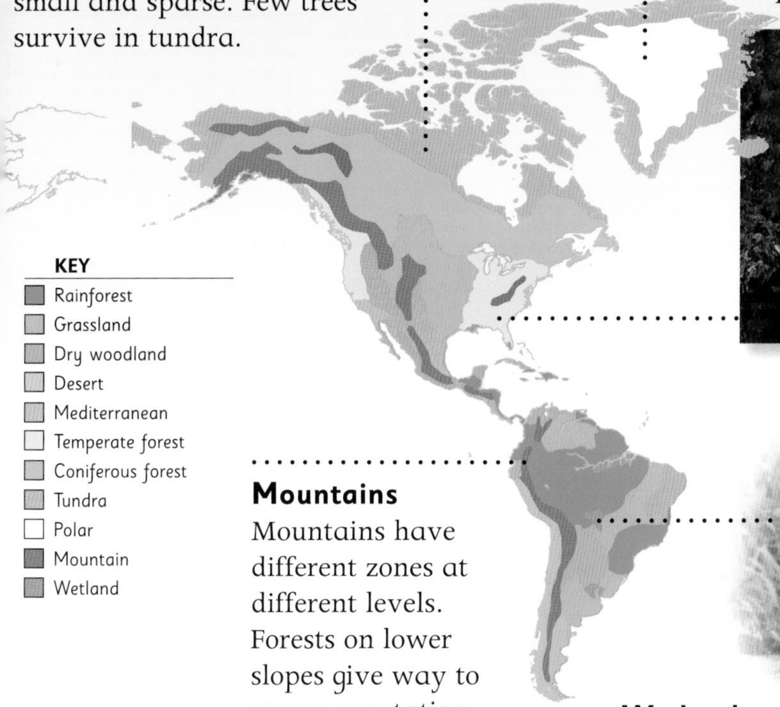

KEY
- ■ Rainforest
- ▨ Grassland
- ▧ Dry woodland
- □ Desert
- ▨ Mediterranean
- □ Temperate forest
- ▨ Coniferous forest
- ▨ Tundra
- □ Polar
- ▨ Mountain
- ▨ Wetland

Mountains

Mountains have different zones at different levels. Forests on lower slopes give way to sparse vegetation and colder air temperatures.

Wetlands

The ground in a wetland is covered in water, making the ground permanently spongy. Birdlife thrives in wetlands.

Prairies, savannas, pampas, and steppes.

Ecosystems

Within a biome, there are lots of ecosystems. An ecosystem is the plants and animals that live in a particular area. That area may be a small pond or a meadow or a rotting log, but whatever its size, the living things within it form a community.

A healthy variety

Biodiversity is the name given to the variety of species living in an ecosystem. Biodiversity is important because nothing can survive on its own. In a small area of rainforest, there may be 150 different types of beetle.

Hazelnut weevil

Weevils are a type of beetle.

Ecologists use a square grid (a quadrat) to measure the numbers of a certain species in a small area.

A ready source of food

Every ecosystem has its food chains. Food chains show which organism eats another. They often form complicated networks.

A simple food chain might begin with grass.

Zebras graze on the grass.

Zebras are preyed upon by lions (which also hunt other prey).

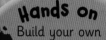

Hands on

Build your own mini ecosystem. Fill a seed tray with potting soil. Create a path with small stones and sprinkle with grass seeds. Water daily. Trim the grass as it grows.

Are Madagascar's forests tropical or temperate?

The geography of plants and animals

A particular biome often contains animals and plants that do not live anywhere else. These are known as "native" species and they have developed special ways of coping with local conditions. Lemurs, for example, are found only on Madagascar.

Seventy per cent of Madagascar's plants and animals are found nowhere else in the world.

Madagascar is the world's fourth largest island. It lies off the south-eastern coast of Africa.

Some of Madagascar's chameleons are tiny.

Sifaka (a type of lemur)

Why only there?

Many animals found on Madagascar came originally from Africa. Millions of years ago, Madagascar was joined to Africa. When the island broke away, its plants and animals were stranded.

A special breed

After Madagascar became a separate island, its animals developed independently. Lemurs did not survive in Africa, but on isolated Madagascar, they did.

Some lemurs move along the ground with a dancing sideways motion.

weird or what?

A foreign species can damage an ecosystem. The cane toad was introduced to Australia to eat beetles in sugar fields, but they have become a pest because they also eat other animals.

Madagascar is home to tropical rainforests.

Polar regions

The Arctic and Antarctic are Earth's coldest and bleakest zones, and few people have visited them. The air is so cold that your breath forms ice crystals, while the Sun's brightness dazzles the naked eye.

The Arctic

The Arctic Ocean is the world's smallest ocean.

The Arctic

The Arctic is a frozen ocean – a huge sheet of floating ice. At the North Pole, this ice stays frozen all the time, but further south the ice melts and begins to break up in the summer months.

The polar bear is the world's largest land predator.

A time-lapse photograph shows how the Arctic Sun doesn't set below the horizon.

A long day

The poles are plunged into total darkness during their winter months, but the Sun doesn't set in the summer. It's a challenging environment, but animals do survive there.

Arctic animals

More animals live in the Arctic than the Antarctic, because winter ice joins the Arctic to Russia and North America.

Narwhal Male narwhals grow a tusk that can reach 2–3 m (7–10 ft) long.

Ribbon seals Adults develop black skin with four white stripes.

Walruses are large marine mammals. They feed on crabs and molluscs.

Iceberg

I spy an iceberg!

In the Arctic, icebergs break off coastal glaciers and flow into the North Atlantic. They move thanks to wind and currents, and melt and break up. Some can take two years to melt.

Which has the largest area of ice, the Arctic or Antarctic?

The Antarctic

There is land underneath Antarctica, but it is covered by 90 per cent of the world's ice, to an average depth of 1.6 km (1 mile).

Antarctica

Freezing winds help to make Antarctica the coldest place on Earth.

Antarctic research station

Humans and the poles

Humans have lived in the Arctic for thousands of years, but there is no evidence they have lived on Antarctica. However, thousands of scientists are based in Antarctica. They live at research stations.

Antarctic animals

No land mammals live on Antarctica, but the ocean is full of animals.

 Weddell seals live further south than any other mammal.

 Orcas are also known as killer whales. They are efficient hunters.

 Humpback whale This whale has the longest flippers of any whale.

 Adélie penguin These small penguins rest on pack ice in winter.

 Sea stars are found on the sea floor under the Antarctic pack ice.

Emperor penguins are the only penguins to breed in winter.

Emperor penguin colony

Emperor penguins are the largest of all penguins. They can grow up to 1 metre (40 inches) tall.

Tundra

Tundra is a type of land that lies mainly around the Arctic Circle, but it is also found near Antarctica and on high mountains. Even in summer, the temperature remains chilly.

A treeless tundra
Look around the tundra and you will notice that there are hardly any trees. That's because the soil is frozen for much of the year, so trees cannot put down deep roots. The few that do grow are stunted and bent by the wind.

The tundra environment

The tundra is cold and windy and receives little rain. The conditions are so harsh that few animals live there all year round. When snow covers the ground, they move south to find food.

The name tundra comes from a Sami (Finnish) word that means "treeless land".

Flowering plants have only a short time to make seeds that will grow next year.

Arctic poppy

Plant life
Most of the land is covered in tough grasses, mosses, heathers, and small shrubs. In spring there is a brief burst of colour as flowers blossom.

Why does the Arctic hare change the colour of its fur in winter?

Under threat

The Arctic tundra is under threat because large amounts of oil and minerals are thought to lie beneath it. Extracting them could damage this fragile ecosystem.

Summer melting

Summer is short on the tundra. As the temperature rises, the water in the top layer of soil melts and forms bogs and small pools. Permanently frozen soil is called permafrost.

Pipelines take gas and oil across large stretches of the Alaskan tundra.

Tundra animals

Life on the tundra is hard, but many animals have adapted to cope:

 Bears migrate to the tundra in summer to feed on plants and berries.

 Musk oxen have long, thick fur that keeps them warm throughout the year.

 Arctic foxes feed mainly on lemmings but will eat anything they can find.

 Lemmings live in burrows and make tunnels under the snow.

 Snowy owls build their nests on hills and ridges instead of in trees.

Arctic hare

The Arctic hare has white fur in winter and brown fur in summer.

Reindeer use their hooves and antlers to reach grass and lichen beneath the snow.

Svalbard reindeer

So that it can blend in against the snow.

Forests

Almost thirty per cent of Earth's land is covered by forests, but they are not all the same. They range from hot and tropical to cool, temperate zones to colder polar regions.

What is temperate?

The word temperate means "not extreme". Temperate zones have warm summers and cool winters. Temperatures never rise to levels found at the equator, and never fall to polar levels either.

Maple forest

Broad, flat leaves are found in temperate zones.

Horse chestnut leaf

Needle-shaped leaves grow on conifers such as spruce and pine.

Pine needles

Types of forest

There are three main types of forest: coniferous, temperate, and tropical.

Coniferous forests

These forests are usually made up of evergreen conifers. Evergreen means they always have leaves.

Temperate forests

Most trees in temperate forests are deciduous, which means they lose their leaves each year. Most leaves are flat.

Tropical forests

Enter a tropical forest and the air is hot and moist. The trees compete for space, and there are plenty of animals.

Where are the tallest trees in the world?

Forest leaves in temperate zones change their colours in autumn.

Count the rings!

Forest life

All forests are filled with an amazing variety of life.

Bears can be found in some forests. Most eat berries and fruits.

Fungi can be found feeding on dead wood in temperate forests.

Beetles are important for breaking down dead and decaying material.

Flowers found in forests have to survive living in shade and semi shade.

Kiwis are flightless birds found only in New Zealand.

Leafcutter ants cut leaves and use them to farm a form of fungus.

How to date a tree

As a tree begins its period of growth each year, it adds a new layer of wood to its trunk. If a tree is felled, the number of rings tells you the age of the tree.

Our demand for wood has a huge impact on forests.

Trees and people

People have cleared forests to use the land for thousands of years. Timber is also in great demand, for use as fuel, and for planks for buildings and furniture.

Ongoing use

Bark is harvested from the cork oak every nine years to supply cork that is used as stoppers in wine bottles, for sea floats, and for notice boards.

weird or what?

Scientists studying one tree in Peru found 43 ant species. That's about the same number of ant species as are found in the whole of England.

55

In California, USA, the coast redwoods grow more than 100 m (330 ft) tall.

Rainforests

Rainforests are some of the wettest places on the planet. They get at least 180 cm (71 in) of rain a year, which helps trees grow tall and fast. The tallest trees in the world grow in rainforests.

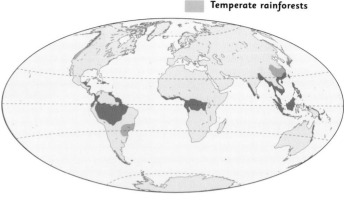

■ Tropical rainforests
■ Temperate rainforests

Tropical or temperate?

Everyone thinks of rainforests as being hot and steamy, but they can also be cool and cloudy. The largest areas of rainforest are in the tropics, which lie in a band around the equator. Temperate rainforests are found along the coast in cooler countries.

Emergent layer tree

Clouds of water vapour rise from tropical rainforests because the air is hot and holds a lot of water. When it cools it falls back down as rain.

Lungs of the world

Rainforests are sometimes called the lungs of the world. This is because trees take in vast amounts of carbon dioxide from the atmosphere and give out oxygen. This process (called photosynthesis) prevents carbon dioxide building up and warming the planet.

What are these colourful, big-beaked birds called?

Rainforest layers

Tropical rainforests are divided into four layers. Each provides a home for different types of animals and plants.

Emergent layer The tallest trees can reach heights of up to 55 m (180 ft) and are home to eagles, bats, and butterflies.

Canopy This thick layer of foliage is full of animals, birds, and climbing plants.

Understorey Small trees and shrubs provide cover for small animals and predators.

Forest floor This is the darkest part of the forest where fungi help break down decaying plant matter.

Creatures of the forest

Rainforests are home to nearly half the world's species of animals, including:

 Jaguars are stealthy predators that blend into the background.

 Toucans use their colourful beaks to reach for fruit and nuts.

 Orangutans swing through the forests of Southeast Asia.

 Tree frogs rarely leave the canopy, except to breed or lay eggs.

 Spiders are big in the rainforest – some eat small birds and frogs.

 Butterflies are attracted by the colourful flowers that grow in the tropics.

 Okapi are shy animals that live deep in the African rainforest.

Huge flocks of parrots live in the South American rainforest.

Under threat

Many plant and animal species live in rainforests but these areas are under threat from people cutting down the trees for wood or clearing land to grow crops. We may even be losing species before we have discovered them.

Macaws. They are members of the parrot family.

The North American prairies

Grasslands

Imagine a sea of grass ahead of you, gently swaying in the wind. A lone tree breaks up the horizon, and a herd of animals is quietly grazing. Nearby a group of large predators is hunting, eyes locked on the herd. Welcome to the African savanna!

A grass landscape

Wild grasses once covered huge areas of Earth's land, but farming has reduced this. Grasses succeed where there is too little rainfall to support trees, but enough to prevent a desert forming.

Grasslands are rich grazing grounds for herbivores.

Zebra

Wildebeest

What's in a name?

Grasslands have different names in different areas of the world. In Africa they are known as savannas, in Russia as steppes. North American grasslands are prairies, while in South America they are known as pampas.

More than just grass

Grasslands are full of wildflowers, including sunflowers, clovers, coneflowers, blazing stars, goldenrods, and asters.

Prairie grasses and flowers in Custer State Park, South Dakota, USA.

A brief fire can help to maintain an area of grassland.

If there are few trees in grasslands, where do birds build their nests?

Grasses

There are many more types of grasses than you might at first think.

Wheat or barley Farmed cereal crops were originally wild grasses.

Buffalo grass is short and hardy. It is found on the plains of North America.

Triodia is a grass that covers large parts of the Australian bush.

Meadow foxtail This grass's spiky seeds attach to passing animals.

Red oat grass is common in East Africa, as well as in Asia and Australia.

Tropical grasslands

It is hot all year round on these grasslands, with a dry season followed by a wet season. The African savanna and the South American pampas are tropical grasslands.

African savannas are broken up by the odd tree.

Temperate grasslands

These grasslands see hot summers and cold winters. Rain falls throughout the year, but not enough to support trees or shrubs. Temperate grasslands include the Russian steppes and North American prairies.

Thomson's gazelle

Grass makes up 90 per cent of a gazelle's diet.

Fire! Fire!

Although they look damaging, controlled fires have been used for centuries to burn off dead growth in grassland, and leave space for new growth.

In burrows.

Deserts

Some deserts are very hot and some deserts are very cold, but there are three things that all deserts have in common: strong sunshine, wind, and very little water.

Become an expert...

on the living world, pages 42-43

on erosion, pages 26-27

Types of desert

Hot deserts can be extremely hot during the day, but at night the temperature can fall to below freezing. This is because there are no clouds in the sky to keep the heat in.

Cold deserts change with the seasons. They are hot in the summer, but in the winter it's cold enough for snow to fall during the day.

Coastal deserts lie where the land meets the ocean. Some oceans have cold currents that make the desert air colder and drier.

Elephant rock, Nevada, USA

Where does sand come from?

Deserts are windy because there are few trees to slow the wind. Huge gusts pick up sand and this wears away (erodes) the surface of any rock, creating strangely shaped rocks and more sand. It takes millions of years for wind to grind rock into sand.

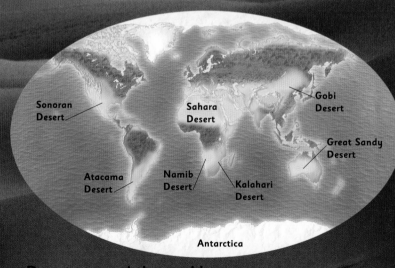

Sonoran Desert

Sahara Desert

Gobi Desert

Great Sandy Desert

Atacama Desert

Namib Desert

Kalahari Desert

Antarctica

Deserts around the world

More than a quarter of Earth's land is made up of deserts. Many of the world's large deserts are on or near to the equator – the imaginary line that runs across the centre of the world.

How big is the Sahara?

Oasis

Scattered in hot deserts are pools of water, called oases. An oasis is where water rises in a spring. It's a place where plants can grow, and animals come to drink, eat the plants, and find shade.

A palm tree can live for well over 100 years.

Less than 25 cm (10 in) of rain falls in a desert in a year.

The Sahara

The Sahara is the world's largest hot desert, covering nearly the whole of North Africa. It is mostly made up of rocks, gravel, and sand. Not many plants can grow there because of the lack of water, and not many animals live in deserts because there aren't enough plants to eat.

Camel

Desert life

The animals and plants that live in a desert have special ways of coping with the shortage of water.

Cacti store water in their stems. The stems stretch to take in water.

Palm trees can often be found next to an oasis. They have few leaves.

Fennec fox This mammal's big ears help it to lose heat.

Thorny devil Spines allow this lizard to collect morning dew to drink.

Jerboas move under the ground in the heat of the day, emerging at night.

People live in deserts too, usually moving around to find supplies.

9,100,000 square km (3,500,000 square miles).

Wetlands

Do you know of a marsh, swamp, or bog or perhaps just a waterlogged area in local woodland? If water lies on soil and cannot drain, it builds up and a wetland develops. Wetlands cover about six per cent of Earth's surface.

The world's largest wetland

… is the Pantanal in South America. Its name comes from a Portuguese word "pântano", which means bog, marsh, or wetland. It covers a huge area.

The Pantanal

Floods regularly cover the ground in the Pantanal.

Types of wetlands

There are many types of wetland. Some of the names you may hear are:

Bog The ground isn't submerged, but is soaked and spongy. Mosses thrive.

Swamp These are wooded areas that are submerged in freshwater or saltwater.

Marsh Plants such as grasses and rushes grow in soggy ground in marshes.

Shallow water wetlands These areas are covered by shallow water.

What lives there?

Around 1,000 types of birds make their home in the Pantanal as well as 400 types of fish and 300 mammal species. Mammals include the world's largest rodent, the capybara.

Capybara

The Yacare caiman makes its home in the Pantanal wetlands.

Wetlands can be saltwater, or fresh

Caiman

Can you name any other rodents that live in wetlands?

Nature's paradise

Wetlands are fabulous environments for water-loving plants and animals. One of the most famous wetlands is Botswana's Okavango Delta.

Aerial shot of Okavango Delta, Botswana

Living in the delta

Wildlife in the delta includes crocodiles, flamingos, and the lechwe, an antelope. These have long hind legs to help them cross marshy ground.

Rice plant

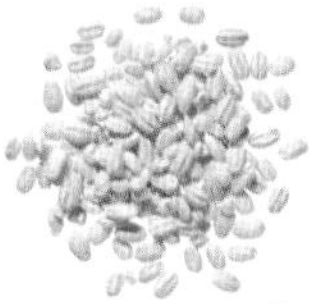

Rice

Rice is a seed. It can be grown on hillside terraces, as shown above.

Wetlands and people

One of the world's most important crops is grown on managed wetlands: rice. Rice feeds around half the world's population.

weird or what?

Wetlands are amazing natural water filters. Sediments and harmful bacteria are removed as water passes through, cleaning the water before it enters streams and rivers.

water, or brackish (a mixture of both).

Water lilies in the Pantanal, Brazil

The beaver, muskrat, coypu, and marsh rat.

The oceans

Five connected oceans lie in hollows (or basins) in Earth's crust: the Pacific, Atlantic, Indian, Southern, and Arctic.

That lives there!

Most life in the world's oceans is to be found around the continents. The ocean can be divided into distinct zones.

Tidal zone This is the land between high and low tide. Creatures here burrow into the sand or mud, or attach themselves to rocks.

Sunlit zone 0–200 metres (0–650 ft). This is where most ocean life is to be found. The waters prove a rich feeding ground for predators.

Twilight zone 200–2,000 metres (650–6,500 ft). Light fades the lower you go, until at about 1,000 metres (3,280 ft) it is dark. Sperm whales hunt squid in this zone.

Deepsea zone 2,000–10,000 metres (6,500–33,000 ft). Deep down, the water is very cold and there is no light. But there is life, including gulper eels and anglerfish.

Can you name some creatures that live in a tidal zone?

At the bottom of the food web

All ocean life depends on plankton, tiny organisms that drift in the oceans. They can be divided into phytoplankton (plants) and zooplankton (animals).

Orca

Sea lion

Lemonfish

Herring

Zooplankton

Phytoplankton

North Sea
Average depth 94 m (308 ft)

Arctic Ocean
Average depth 1,050 m (3,445 ft)

Mediterranean Sea
Average depth 1,500 m (4,921 ft)

How deep?

Oceans and seas vary enormously in depth. The world's deepest is the icy Southern Ocean.

Caribbean Sea
Average depth 2,647 m (8,684 ft)

Atlantic Ocean
Average depth 3,330 m (10,925 ft)

Indian Ocean
Average depth 3,890 m (12,762 ft)

Pacific Ocean
Average depth 4,280 m (14,040 ft)

Southern Ocean
Average depth 4,500 m (14,800 ft)

People and the ocean

As well as making use of its salt, people have fished from the oceans for thousands of years.

Plankton in bloom

In the right conditions, plankton multiply in huge numbers and can be spotted on satellite photographs.

Small fishing trawler

Plankton bloom off the coast of France

65

Among many others, there are crabs, shellfish, sea stars, sea urchins, and worms.

Down to earth

Grab a fistful of soil, and what are you holding? Healthy soil contains rock fragments, minerals, dead plants and animals, lots of microscopic creatures (and some that are not so microscopic!), oxygen, bacteria, fungi, and water.

The richer the soil, the healthier the plants.

The top level is the topsoil. This level is rich in food and contains lots of living creatures.

A story of layers

If you could cut a section through the soil you walk on, you would see that it is made up of layers. Soil sits on solid rock, and above that it normally gets richer the closer to the surface it gets.

Below the topsoil, the subsoil has a lot less goodness.

Lower still, the soil is rockier.

Wriggle, wriggle

Worms are vital for healthy soil. They feast on decaying plants and animals as they move through the soil, making the soil richer with their waste. They also create tunnels, which helps the soil to "breathe".

The solid rock base is called "bedrock".

What is the name for scientists who study soil?

Compost is good!

Why add rotting vegetable waste to a compost bin? As this waste breaks down, it releases valuable nutrients, encouraging earthworms and creating a rich compost for growing plants.

Add vegetable peelings and eggshells to a compost bin. But cooked vegetables won't break down.

Soil separation

Soil settles naturally into layers – try it yourself. You will need a lidded plastic container. Add two-thirds water, then enough soil to almost fill it. Shake, then leave it to settle.

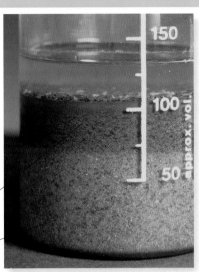

A layer of silt settles above finer sand particles.

The heavier, larger particles of sand will settle at the bottom of the container.

Hands on

Soil is alive with tiny creatures. Sink an empty yogurt pot into the ground so the rim is level with the soil's surface. Leave overnight and see what creatures fall into it.

A teaspoon of soil may contain up to one billion micro-organisms.

Different soils

Not all soils are the same. You can feel the difference, depending on the amounts of:

Sand Large particles with sharp edges make sandy soil feel gritty to touch.

Silt Rubbed between your fingers, this soil feels silky and soft, rather like flour.

Clay These are the smallest particles in soil. Clay gets sticky when wet.

Is soil important?

Soil is one of the most important things around you. Without it, we could not survive as we need plants for food and plants need soil in which to grow – they extract water from soil through a branching network of roots. A plant's root system also holds it upright.

Scientists who study soil are called pedologists.

People and the planet

Geography is not just about the physical processes that shape our world. It is also about the people who live in it.

Strip mining for minerals creates huge holes in the ground.

Shaping the planet

People have had a great effect on our planet. We have flattened mountains, diverted rivers, and cut down forests. We have built skyscrapers, dams, roads, and bridges. Everything humans make or do has an impact on our world.

Human activity
Humans have adapted to live in all environments, from hot deserts to icy plains. To survive, we have learned to live together in groups. These vary in size from small villages to large towns and cities.

Where is Antarctica?

World of difference

Every continent is divided up into countries. Each country is different, as are the people that live there. They all have separate cultures, languages, religions, and ideas about what it means to be a part of that country.

Unoccupied territory

There is only one place in the world that is not divided into countries – Antarctica. Seven countries (France, Norway, New Zealand, Argentina, Chile, Australia, and the UK) have laid claim to part of it but, under a treaty, Antarctica is protected from development.

There's nobody here but us penguins – and a few research scientists.

Curiosity quiz

Look through the Human Geography pages and see if you can identify the picture clues below.

Become an expert...

on what makes a country, pages **70-71**

on cultural celebrations, page **100**

It is the continent at the South Pole.

What is a country?

Northern Ireland

If someone asks where you come from, what do you say – Spain, France, India, China? We all live in a particular geographical area that we call a country.

How many countries?

There are 195 independent countries in the world. This is not the full total as some countries are governed by another country.

Capital cities
Each country has a capital city. This is usually where the government of the country is based, but it is not always the largest or most active city.

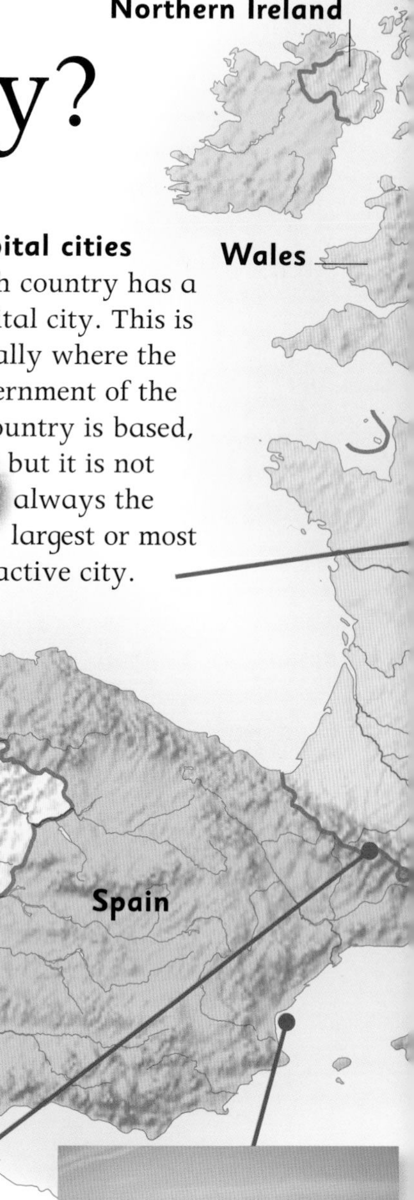

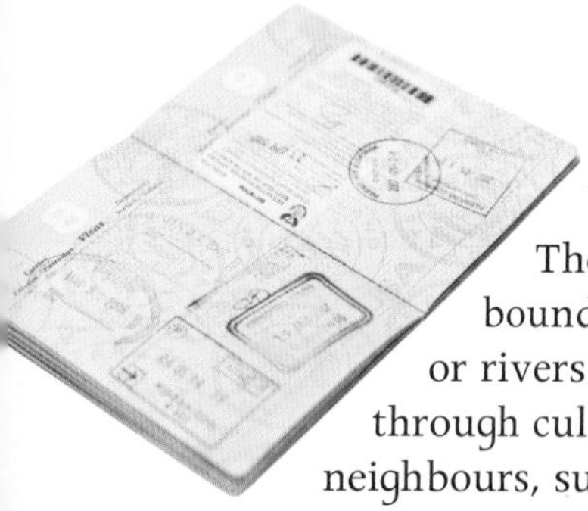

Wales

On the border
Each country is separated by boundaries called borders. These can be physical boundaries, such as coastlines or rivers. Others have come about through cultural differences with neighbours, such as language or religion.

Spain

Mountain borders
Mountain ranges make obvious boundaries. The Pyrenees are a chain of mountains that form a natural border between Spain and France.

Coasts
Coastlines are the easiest physical borders to see. Countries also claim a short distance out to sea as part of their territory.

70

What is the name of the tower in the middle of Paris shown above?

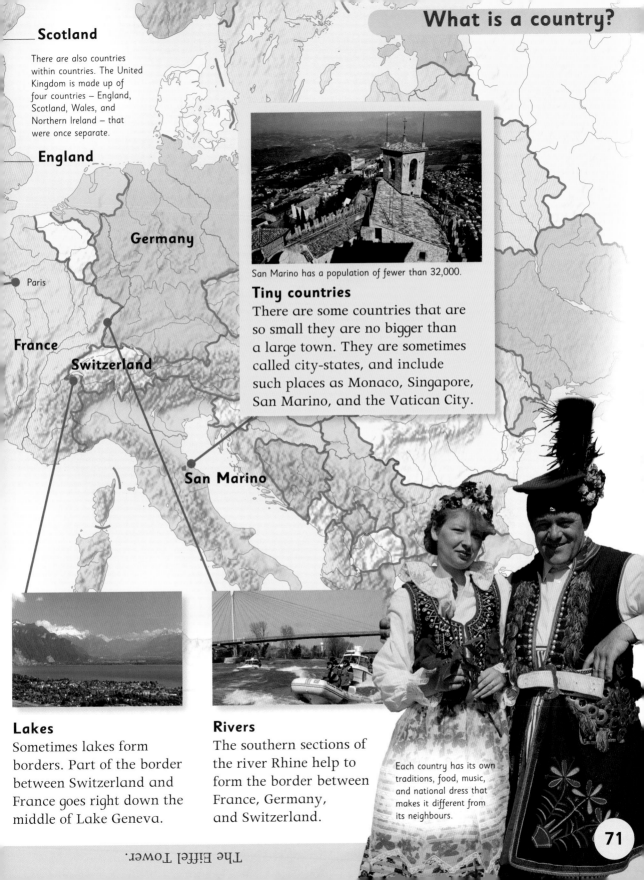

Scotland

There are also countries within countries. The United Kingdom is made up of four countries – England, Scotland, Wales, and Northern Ireland – that were once separate.

England

Paris

Germany

France

Switzerland

San Marino has a population of fewer than 32,000.

Tiny countries

There are some countries that are so small they are no bigger than a large town. They are sometimes called city-states, and include such places as Monaco, Singapore, San Marino, and the Vatican City.

San Marino

Lakes

Sometimes lakes form borders. Part of the border between Switzerland and France goes right down the middle of Lake Geneva.

Rivers

The southern sections of the river Rhine help to form the border between France, Germany, and Switzerland.

Each country has its own traditions, food, music, and national dress that makes it different from its neighbours.

Rural or urban?

Do you live in the countryside with open land around you (a rural area), or in a town or a city (an urban area)?

From small beginnings

A thousand years ago, most of the world's population lived in small settlements. They were farmers, scratching a living from the land as best they could.

Half and half

Overall, just under half the world's population now live in rural areas and just over half in urban areas, but proportions vary from country to country. In many African countries, most of the population still live in rural areas. In Europe, most people live in urban areas.

weird or what?

Major cities have populations in the millions, but there are also small cities. The smallest city in the United Kingdom, St Davids, Wales, boasts a population of just 1,600.

Which city has the most people?

Thinking big

Today, many people still work the land, but many have powerful equipment to help them and the fields they farm are far bigger than in the past. That's because they supply huge markets: the cities.

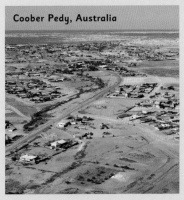

Coober Pedy, Australia

So does "rural" mean farmland?

No! Rural areas are not just made up of farms and the land surrounding them. They may be forests, open grassland, plains, deserts, – these are all areas where people choose to live.

City transportation depends on a network of railway lines.

Somewhere in the middle

Lots of people live in suburban areas, which are areas of housing that spread out around cities and towns. The people living here will often travel, or commute, into the city centres to work.

Tokyo, which has a population of more than 37 million people.

Living on the coast

Everybody loves to go to the seaside, but the coast is not just a place to enjoy yourself. Coastal towns and cities are vital to industry and trade with the rest of the world.

Cities on the sea

More than half of the world's population lives on the coast. In fact, more than 70 per cent of the biggest cities in the world are situated near the sea, and the numbers of people and cities are set to grow.

More than 11,563,000 people live in Rio de Janeiro, Brazil's largest and most popular coastal city.

These houses are in danger of falling into the sea as waves slowly erode the cliff edges.

Fringes of the land

Coasts are where the land meets the sea. The land may slope gently to the sea or drop abruptly from steep cliffs. The sea is so powerful that the shape of the coastline can change every year.

Which city in Brazil gets the most visitors?

Shipping is vital for sending goods out to other parts of the world and bringing in things we need.

Coastal industries

Many industries rely on the sea. Fishing and shipping are important ways of making money for many countries. They are usually located in places where there is deep enough water for a harbour or port.

Fishing provides local jobs and food that can be sent all around the country.

Visitor attraction

The coast is a great place to visit. Some people go to swim, others like fishing, boating, or walking. Local industries spring up to support these activities — boat yards, hotels, shops, campsites, and restaurants.

Teaching people to surf is only a summer job in many coastal resorts.

Human impact

Humans have a huge impact on the coast. Building houses and hotels, dredging the sea floor, and pollution can all damage the fragile ecosystem. This may have an effect on people who depend on the sea for a living.

Become an expert...

on erosion, pages **26-27**

on tourism, pages **98-99**

The Palm in Dubai is a luxury resort that has been built out into the sea.

Town planning

Do you have to travel far to reach a local shop or a doctor, or are these services just a stroll away? If you live in a town or city, a lot of planning will have gone into where these services are placed.

This model was built to show the plans for a new town in China.

Let's park there

Road networks and car park provisions are big considerations for town planners. Many people now own a car. Shopping centres all need car parks – and it takes a lot of planning to get everything coordinated and working smoothly.

Multi-storey car park

Hands on

Why not sketch your own plans for a town! You'll find there's a lot to think about. How big should the buildings be? How many parks are needed? Have fun!

How my town would look!

Name seven essentials for a new city.

Who's involved?

If a new town is being planned, all sorts of people will contribute ideas and plans, including:

Environmental planners suggest ways in which the environment can be protected, perhaps with parks.

Architects develop detailed drawings, plans, and 3-D models for homes, schools, and offices.

Engineers advise on the materials available for building a structure safely and within budget.

Transport planners look into the transport networks needed for people to travel to work and school.

Let's get planning!

The following developments are all essential considerations if a new large town is being planned.

 Schools Children need schools, and that means space has to be set aside for the buildings.

 Hospitals A large hospital may serve thousands of people. A large city will require several hospitals.

 Leisure centres People need entertainment. A leisure centre brings lots of sport activities together.

 Shops Today, many cities have huge shopping centres, but smaller shops remain popular.

We don't want that!

Planning issues create strong feelings. The need for new housing will often concern local residents. That's why a new school, for example, can take a long time from planning to finished building.

New building work means lots of diggers.

77

Houses, schools, doctor's surgeries, offices, leisure centres, and shops.

Linking it all up

Do you catch a bus to school?
Is the apple you eat grown
locally? Whether it is moving
you from place to place, or
your food, we affect our world
by our transport needs.

The demand for road
transport leads to
long traffic jams.

On the water

Canals were used
in some countries
to transport goods
long before the
invention of trains
and aeroplanes.

All at sea

Shipping routes have been used for
thousands of years, creating networks
for trade and the spread of ideas.

Large ships still
transport huge
quantities of goods.

On the road

Lorries fill our
roads, delivering
goods from food
and furniture to
livestock and
clothes. People seek
out the fastest
route – large roads
are built as straight
as possible.

Like ancient
Roman roads,
major routes
between cities are
built as straight
as they can be.

A busy road junction directs traffic
safely and avoids delays.

Name the four methods of transport.

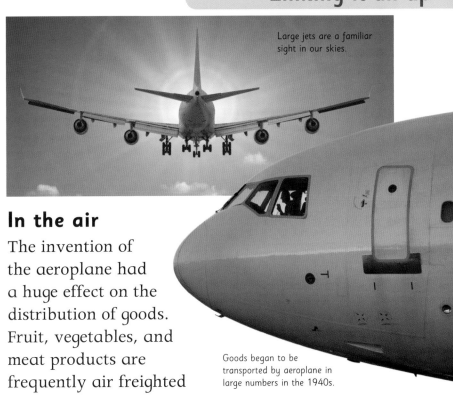

Large jets are a familiar sight in our skies.

In the air

The invention of the aeroplane had a huge effect on the distribution of goods. Fruit, vegetables, and meat products are frequently air freighted enormous distances.

Goods began to be transported by aeroplane in large numbers in the 1940s.

A freight train is long... possibly up to 3 km (2 miles) long!

Transporting goods by train

You may think that air freight is the major mover of goods, but goods trains deliver all sorts of things, from post and grain to cars and coal. In the USA, railways account for more than 40 per cent of all freight transportation.

수원 → 기흥부근
12km 정체

79

By road, by rail, by air, and by water.

Structures

Nature has created many incredible structures – caves, arches, islands, and lakes. But humans have put their mark on the landscape by building structures that are as amazing as anything in the natural world.

The only way is up

How do you fit a lot of people into a building if you only have a small site? The answer is to build a skyscraper. The highest tower in the world is the Burj Khalifa in Dubai. Around 12,000 people are expected to live and work there.

The Burj Khalifa tower stands 828 m (2,717 ft) high.

Ancient structures

Not all of our greatest structures are new. Here are some we made earlier:

 Pyramids were being built in Egypt about 4,500 years ago.

 The Taj Mahal in India is an elaborate tomb made of white marble.

 The Colosseum was built in 80 CE by the Romans to hold gladiator contests.

 Stonehenge in England is an ancient stone circle used to celebrate midsummer.

 Angkor Wat in Cambodia is a Hindu temple made from carved sandstone.

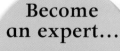

Become an expert...

on transport, pages 78-79
on living in cities, pages 72-73

What is a strait?

Vehicle Assembly Building

The largest single-storey building is the Vehicle Assembly Building at Cape Canaveral in Florida, USA. It is where rockets and the space shuttle are put together for launch. The building is so huge it even has its own weather – small clouds form inside on humid days.

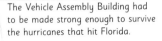
The Vehicle Assembly Building had to be made strong enough to survive the hurricanes that hit Florida.

The "Crystal Cathedral", USA

Crystal palaces

Glass is often used to build light and airy structures such as skyscrapers and airports. This church has 10,000 panes of glass, but can withstand a severe earthquake.

The Millau Bridge in France seems to float above the clouds.

The Akashi Kaikyo Bridge links the islands of Honshu and Awaji. The Akashi Strait is nearly 6.5 km (4 miles) wide where the bridge crosses it.

Crossings

Bridges are used to cross large expanses of water or land. The longest single-span suspension bridge is the Akashi Kaikyo Bridge in Japan. Its central section is 1,991 m (6,532 ft) long. The tallest bridge is the Millau Bridge in France. At 343 m (1,125 ft), it is taller than the Eiffel Tower.

It is a narrow channel of water.

Changing places

The landscape around us is changing constantly. Over time, humans have altered the areas where they live by building towns and factories, cutting down woodlands, and farming, but there is always a bit of history left behind.

This ruined church is usually hidden beneath the waters of a Spanish reservoir.

Buried information

If you look down from a helicopter or aeroplane you often get clues about how the landscape used to look. Sometimes you can see the remains of ancient buildings buried beneath the soil.

Under the water

Reservoirs are man-made lakes that are built to provide a water supply. Often they involve damming a river so that it floods a valley. Any villages in the valley become submerged, but are revealed when the water level drops.

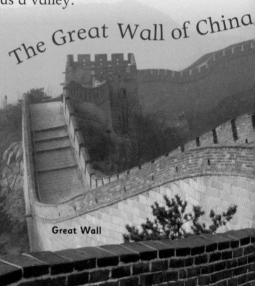

The Great Wall of China

Great Wall

The Great Wall used to mark the border between China and countries to the north

What is the name of the wall that used to divide England and Scotland?

In Roman times, Pompeii and Herculaneum were completely destroyed when the volcano Mount Vesuvius erupted and buried the towns in ash.

Tracing the past

Any place that humans have lived reveals traces of its past. Different types of houses show how and when a town grew. Street names such as Church Road or Factory Lane tell you something about what was built or used to happen in that area.

Lost places

Sometimes places vanish from the map. War, famine, and disease can make people abandon towns and villages forever. Natural disasters, such as earthquakes or floods, can also reduce cities to ruins.

This shop sign was dug out of the ash in Pompeii.

If you look around any town you can see that some buildings are much older than others.

is 8,850 km (5,500 miles) long.

Boundary changes

What did the outline of your country look like 100 or 1,000 years ago? It is likely that its borders have changed in some way through conquest, or agreement with a neighbour over where the edge of each country should be. See if you can find an old map to compare borders with a modern map.

Become an expert...
on what makes a border, pages **70-71**
on town planning, pages **76-77**

Hadrian's Wall. It was named after a Roman emperor.

People planet

Each minute, somewhere in the world, there are around 255 births and 100 deaths. What does that mean? It means that the human population is rising. In fact, each year the world's population increases by about 74 million people.

Demand for land
It's thought that about half of all Earth's available land has been altered for human use – whether by farming, forestry, housing, or industry.

Become an expert...
on town planning, pages **76-77**
on languages, pages **86-87**

Population and geography
Where this growing population chooses to live affects the world around them, especially if they group together in towns or cities. Cities attract huge numbers with their promise of work.

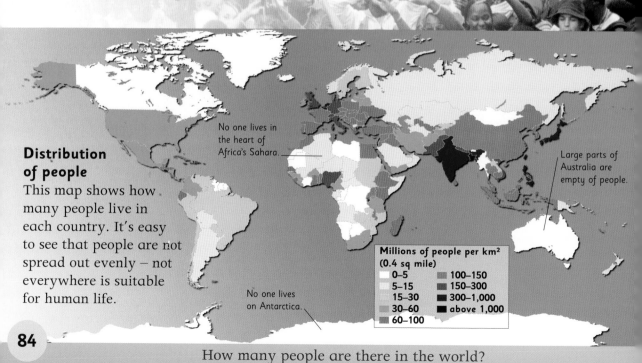

Distribution of people
This map shows how many people live in each country. It's easy to see that people are not spread out evenly – not everywhere is suitable for human life.

No one lives in the heart of Africa's Sahara.

Large parts of Australia are empty of people.

No one lives on Antarctica.

Millions of people per km² (0.4 sq mile)
0–5	100–150
5–15	150–300
15–30	300–1,000
30–60	above 1,000
60–100	

How many people are there in the world?

How long do people live?

This is called a person's life expectancy and it varies widely from country to country. It depends on that country's health care and nutrition, as well as people's access to water.

About one-sixth of the world's population does not have access to clean water.

One of the world's biggest killers is a disease called malaria, spread by the mosquito.

Population growth

Populations are expanding faster than they used to because a better diet and better health care has led to falling death rates. Not only do people live longer, but children also have a better chance of survival.

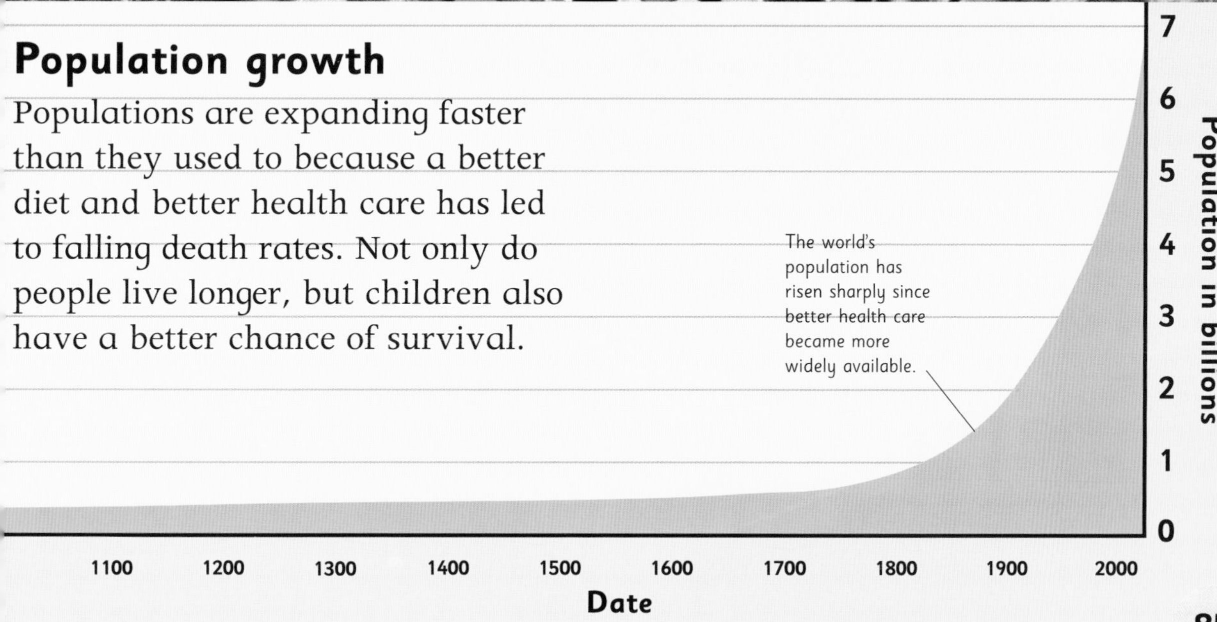

The world's population has risen sharply since better health care became more widely available.

Population in billions

7
6
5
4
3
2
1
0

Date

1100 1200 1300 1400 1500 1600 1700 1800 1900 2000

85

In 2010, the world's population stood at 6.8 billion.

Geography of language

How many languages do you speak?
Just one, or two, or even three?
Did you know that there
are almost 7,000
recognized
languages?

Who speaks what?

It is possible to show languages
spoken on a map of the world,
as here, but remember that
these languages are also spoken
elsewhere. Also, millions of people
can speak two or more languages.

In Canada, the
people of Québec
province mostly
speak French.

This map cannot show all
the languages spoken within
a country, but it shows the
language most widely spoken
or understood.

Millions of people

Did you know?

It is estimated that around
half of the world's languages
will disappear in the next 100
years – many are spoken by
tiny numbers of people, and
children no longer
learn them.

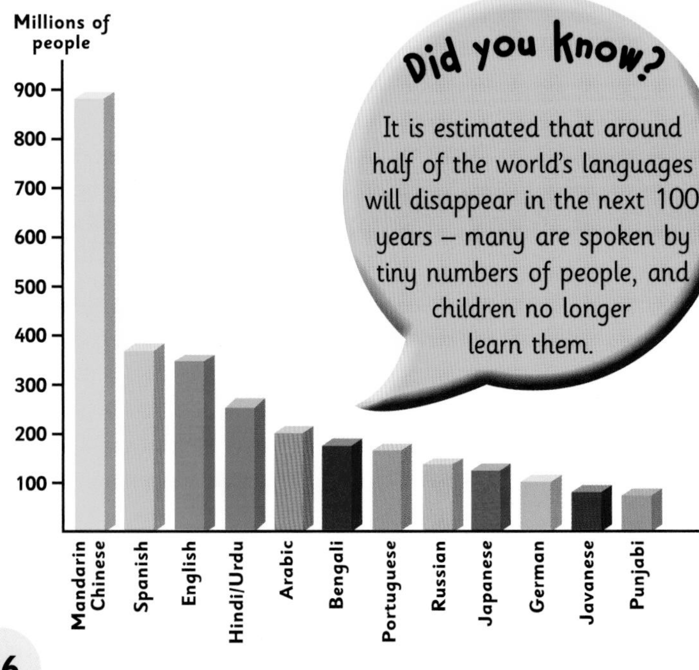

900
800
700
600
500
400
300
200
100

Mandarin Chinese | Spanish | English | Hindi/Urdu | Arabic | Bengali | Portuguese | Russian | Japanese | German | Javanese | Punjabi

Language spoken

This graph shows the languages that
have the most speakers who use that
language as their first language.

Looking at the graph, how many millions of people speak Mandarin Chinese?

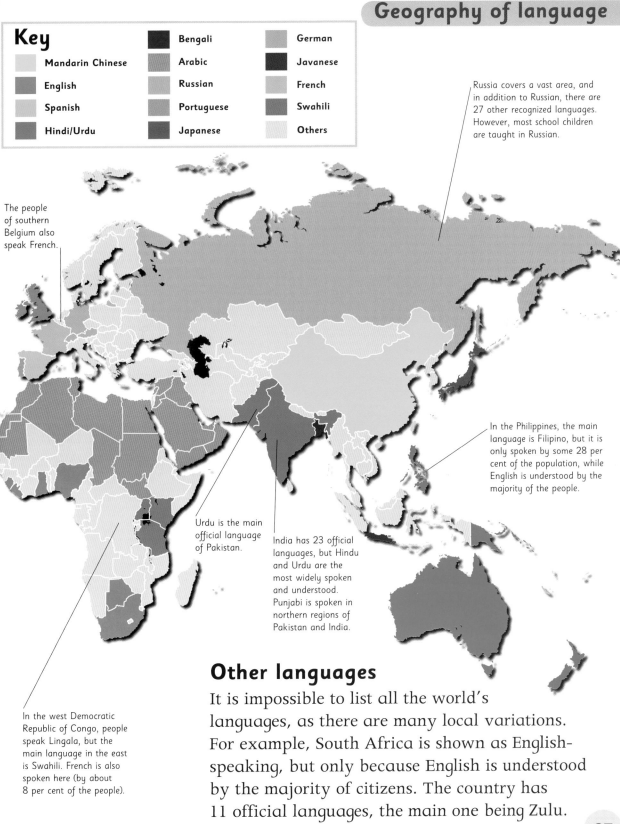

Key

- Mandarin Chinese
- English
- Spanish
- Hindi/Urdu
- Bengali
- Arabic
- Russian
- Portuguese
- Japanese
- German
- Javanese
- French
- Swahili
- Others

Russia covers a vast area, and in addition to Russian, there are 27 other recognized languages. However, most school children are taught in Russian.

The people of southern Belgium also speak French.

In the Philippines, the main language is Filipino, but it is only spoken by some 28 per cent of the population, while English is understood by the majority of the people.

Urdu is the main official language of Pakistan.

India has 23 official languages, but Hindu and Urdu are the most widely spoken and understood. Punjabi is spoken in northern regions of Pakistan and India.

In the west Democratic Republic of Congo, people speak Lingala, but the main language in the east is Swahili. French is also spoken here (by about 8 per cent of the people).

Other languages

It is impossible to list all the world's languages, as there are many local variations. For example, South Africa is shown as English-speaking, but only because English is understood by the majority of citizens. The country has 11 official languages, the main one being Zulu.

87

An estimated 880 million people use Mandarin Chinese as their first language.

A country's resources

Every country needs something that can be traded for money or goods. The most basic goods are those that grow or are found naturally. We call these "resources".

Minerals

Minerals are substances that occur in the ground and have to be extracted by mining or quarrying. The most useful are metals, such as iron, tin, and copper.

One mineral that is mined and used all over the world is salt.

Food production

A country's landscape and climate can create the right conditions to grow and produce certain foods, from cattle and sheep for meat to grain such as wheat and rice.

Cattle are raised for meat and dairy products, as well as for leather.

Wood and timber

Trees are a major resource in some parts of the world. They can be specially grown and cut for timber that is then used for building or for making paper.

Trailers stacked with tree trunks, ready for transportation to a timber mill.

Water

Water is a vital resource. Not only is it needed for drinking and to water crops, but it is also used to generate power in hydroelectric plants. Many industries also need water.

Although there is plenty of water on Earth, some places have more than others.

Energy

Coal, oil, and gas are fossil fuels, used to produce heat and electricity. Some countries have plenty of these resources, which they sell to countries that do not.

In some countries, wind or solar power is used as an energy source.

People

The most valuable resource a country has is its people. They may be highly skilled or educated and can create new things, or they may provide a huge labour force.

Many factories depend on a large workforce, with each worker having a specific job.

Which two metals are commonly used to make jewellery?

In North America, huge machines
have replaced the work of many people,
making jobs, such as harvesting, faster.
In less-developed countries most harvests
are gathered by hand.

World industry

A country's wealth depends on
what it can produce and sell.
That depends a lot on geography:
a country may have mines because
it is rich in gems, or it may be ideal
for growing a particular crop.

North America

USA produces wheat,
iron, steel, electronics,
cars, and aircraft.

Canada is the world's
largest exporter of wood
(mainly for building).

Mexico is rich in
natural gas and coal.

KEY

- North America
- South America
- Africa
- Europe
- Asia
- Australasia

South America

Brazil produces
one-quarter of the
world's coffee.

Ecuador has a
climate ideal for
tomatoes and bananas.

Argentina is a
major producer
of beef.

What does a country do when it "exports" goods?

Asia

Saudi Arabia, Iraq, and Kuwait produce oil and natural gas.

Japan is known worldwide for its technology.

India and China are centres for mass-produced cars, clothes, and electronics.

Tokyo is home to one of the world's largest stock exchanges.

Europe

Germany is known for its car production and high-tech goods industries.

Finland and Sweden have large forests and export wood.

Norway and Iceland fish.

Australasia

New Zealand exports wool, meat, and dairy products from farming sheep and cattle.

Australia is rich in iron ore, tin, silver, coal, and diamonds.

Papua New Guinea has copper and gold.

Africa

Congo and Zambia produce minerals.

Namibia is a source of copper and tin.

Nigeria, Algeria, and Libya are major sources of oil and natural gas.

South Africa has mines that are rich in gold and diamonds.

It means that country sells its goods to another country.

Working for a living

Work is an important part of everyday life. Work provides a person with the money to buy things and support their family. It also contributes to the wealth of their country.

Types of jobs

The types of jobs people do depends on how developed the country is. In less-developed countries, most people work in low-paid and low-skilled jobs. Developed countries have more workers in jobs that require a high level of skill or education.

Local work

Many people work in industries based on the natural resources of the area. Farming and mining are examples of this type of work.

Brickworks are often based near to sources of clay and fuel for firing.

Forestry – timber and saw mills are usually located close to a forest.

Mining takes place wherever there is a good supply of a mineral.

People will often move

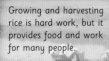
Growing and harvesting rice is hard work, but it provides food and work for many people.

What hard, black mineral is mined for fuel?

Manufacturing

Once the raw materials have been produced they can be made into something else. This is done by industries that turn iron into steel, oil into petrol, and make all the everyday things we need.

Clothes and textiles are made from raw materials like cotton and wool.

Petrol is a product that is processed from crude oil for use in cars.

Household goods include items like pots and pans, furniture, and kettles.

Providing a service

Not all jobs are based on making things. Industries also need transport companies, accountants, and suppliers to keep their businesses going. People also use services such as plumbers, shops, and hairdressers.

Banks handle companies' money, including wages and electronic payments.

Architects design buildings for use as homes and offices.

Bookshops allow you to look at books like this one before you buy them.

Governments are responsible for providing jobs that benefit everybody.

Working for the state

It's not only manufacturers and service industries that provide jobs. Governments collect taxes from people and companies, which they use to pay for schools, hospitals, roads, libraries, emergency services, and other public organizations.

to another town or even another country to find work.

Coal.

Buying and selling

Every country needs to make money to support its people. To do this it has to make things using its natural resources, or provide services that other people pay to use. We call this the economy.

Markets are a good place to sell goods that are made or grown locally.

World economies

Economies work on three scales: local, national, and global. For example:

Local
A dairy farm makes cheese, which it sells in shops and markets in the surrounding area.

National
The dairy farm sells its cheese to a company that sends it to shops around the country.

Global
The dairy farm belongs to an international food company that sells the cheese through its outlets all over the world.

What have you got?

Natural resources are not evenly spread. There is more oil in the Middle East than anywhere else, but there is less land suitable to grow crops. So these countries sell their oil to buy food from overseas.

Which products are in greatest demand around the world?

Trading partners

No country in the world is truly self-sufficient – they all have to trade with other countries for the things they need. Countries sell the things they make best and buy in what they can't produce themselves.

Fish from the Arctic Circle are sent all over the world.

Become an expert...
on world industry, pages **90-91**
on resources, pages **88-89**

Oranges grow best in warm and sunny climates.

Fish

Oranges

Bananas

Bananas grow in the tropical conditions of Central America.

Colombia is a major producer of cut flowers.

Flowers

A fair trade

Producers in developing countries often find it hard to sell their products overseas. Organizations have been set up to make sure that workers in these countries get a fair wage and a good price for their products.

Fair trade products are mainly agricultural crops such as tea, coffee, sugar, fruit juice, cotton, and nuts.

Oil, coffee, steel, gold, and wheat.

95

Waste

Waste is everything we decide that we don't want any more. Waste may be items that we have finished using, or the unwanted materials that are left over after making things we do want. Where does it all go?

Become an expert...

on looking after Earth, pages **40-41**

on resources, pages **88-89**

Out of sight?

Every year, millions of tonnes of rubbish are dumped in landfill and buried in the ground. This is a quick way of getting rid of things we don't want, but it's not the best solution.

We are running out of landfill sites, but much of our waste can be recycled or composted.

What type of creature has its mouth caught in plastic in the picture?

Recycling

Recycling our waste can reduce landfill, protect the environment, and save energy. Lots of things can be recycled and reused, from plastics and paper, to metals and fabrics.

Composting

Rather than throwing it out with the rubbish, we can turn a lot of our kitchen and garden waste into food for plants. It breaks down into a rich soil.

Burning

Some waste is burnt. This reduces the amount of waste being sent to landfill and can be used to create energy to power things such as lights and heating.

It's easy to recycle into separate bins and lots of homes and offices do this.

Things ideal for composting include tea bags, raw fruits and vegetables, and cardboard.

Some people have concerns that burning waste leads to the release of unhealthy chemicals.

A sea of rubbish

Vast quantities of plastics are produced each year. About 10 per cent of this ends up in the oceans, where it collects in calm waters. One such area is the Pacific Garbage Patch in the north Pacific Ocean.

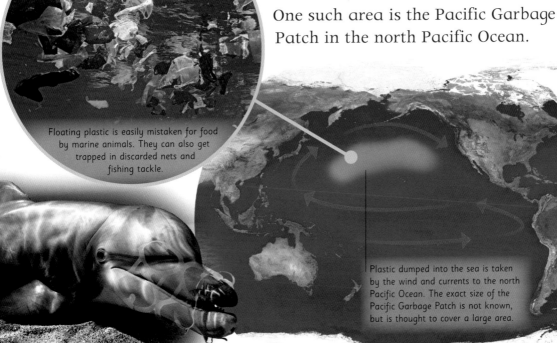

Floating plastic is easily mistaken for food by marine animals. They can also get trapped in discarded nets and fishing tackle.

Plastic dumped into the sea is taken by the wind and currents to the north Pacific Ocean. The exact size of the Pacific Garbage Patch is not known, but is thought to cover a large area.

A bottlenose dolphin.

Going on holiday

There's nothing like visiting somewhere new. Even if it's only a journey to the next town it gives you the opportunity to spend time doing something different, such as trying a completely new culture, food, or lifestyle.

It is estimated that up to half a million people are on an aeroplane at any one time.

Bringing in money

Tourism is a vital industry for many countries. People who visit spend money on air and road travel, accommodation, entertainments, and shopping. Islands, which don't have many natural resources but have sunshine and sandy beaches, find tourism a useful source of income.

Wish you were here!

A business trip

Not all travel is for leisure. Many business people make trips overseas for meetings and conferences. These mainly take place in cities. Good transport links, hotels, and places to eat out are more important to business travellers than beaches and leisure activities.

Where can you ride a camel as shown in the photograph above?

Fun for all

Going away for a holiday was once something only the rich had the time and the money to be able to do. Now, there are cheap and fast ways to travel, including aeroplanes and high-speed railways. These have enabled many more people to travel, for work as well as pleasure.

Let's expand

Tourism can have its problems. If a resort becomes popular it may grow too quickly. This can have impacts on the local area as land is cleared for buildings. It also creates a demand for extra services, such as power and water supplies, as well as transport links.

Local people may be forced off their land to make way for tourists, forcing a change in their way of life.

Fast facts

Millions of people are on holiday right now. Facts about tourism include:

It takes eight days to travel the full distance across Russia on the Trans-Siberian Railway.

The countries that currently receive the most tourists are: France, USA, Spain, China, and Italy.

The world's most visited cities are Paris, London, Kuala Lumpur, Singapore, and New York City.

Space tourism may soon be possible, but the costs are too high for most people.

Some people enjoy visiting countries to see wildlife that they cannot see in their own countries.

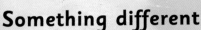

Something different

Nowadays, tourists are looking for something to make their holiday a little bit different. If they have a hobby or interest, they can choose a holiday that includes them. Sports, wildlife, cookery, and archaeological digs are some of the most popular types of activity holiday.

The photograph was taken at ruins in Syria in the Middle East.

Let's celebrate!

People celebrate for all sorts of reasons: it may be religious, it may be historical, or simply the arrival of spring.

Chinese New Year

This is an important Chinese holiday. It lasts 15 days, during which people eat special meals, exchange gifts, and hold processions.

Passover

This is a key Jewish festival. Jews remember when Moses led the Israelites to freedom. It lasts for seven or eight days.

| January | **or** | February | | March | **or** | April | | May | | June |

or   **or**   **or**

Holi

This is celebrated each spring by Hindus and Sikhs, who throw coloured powder and water.

Cherry blossom festival

This is a famous Japanese festival celebrating the beauty of the spring blossoming of cherry trees.

What do many people celebrate each year?

Eid ul Fitr

This Muslim festival marks the end of Ramadan (a month of fasts). It lasts for three days, and starts with a special prayer before the celebrations begin.

Diwali

Also known as the festival of lights, Diwali celebrates the victory of good over evil. Hindu families light oil lamps and share sweets.

Christmas

This is a Christian celebration of the birth of Jesus Christ. People exchange gifts and cards.

or

July	August	September	October	November	December

or

Mid-autumn festival

This celebration of harvest takes place in countries in east Asia. It dates back more than 3,000 years.

Day of the Dead

This is a Mexican festival, when people believe the souls of loved dead relatives return for one night.

Thanksgiving

This North American festival is held on the fourth Thursday of November in the USA and the second Monday in October in Canada. Families give thanks for the first good harvest by European settlers.

The wonderful world of maps

Have you ever had to use a map? A map is an easy way to find your way around, especially if you're travelling to somewhere new.

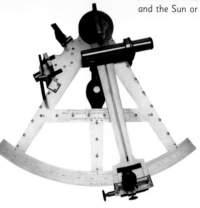

Sextants are still used by some sailors to measure the angle between the horizon and the Sun or a star.

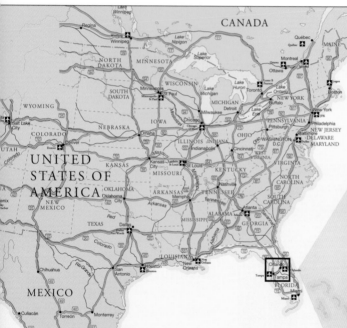

This map shows the eastern side of the USA. Let's zoom in on the part of Florida enclosed by the black square to see how maps work.

The world before maps

For hundreds of years, people had to find their way around using points in the landscape or, if at sea, by using the Sun and stars. Sailors used an instrument called a sextant to work out their position, and a compass to find North.

What is a map?

A map is just like an aerial photograph, but drawn as a diagram. It provides a bird's-eye view of an area. There are all sorts of maps, from road maps and train network maps to nautical charts and street maps.

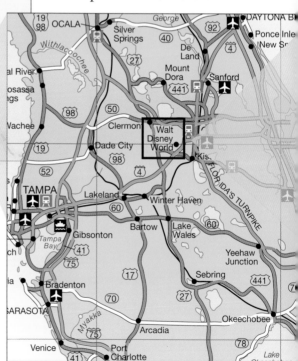

This close-up view shows towns, roads, and interesting places in the area, such as the Disney theme park. Let's zoom in even closer.

What is a mapmaker called?

The wonderful world of maps

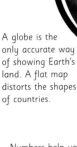

A globe is the only accurate way of showing Earth's land. A flat map distorts the shapes of countries.

A spherical map

A globe is simply a map printed onto a sphere, which represents Earth's shape. The top and bottom of Earth are called the North and South Poles, while the equator runs around the centre.

Curiosity quiz

Look through the World of Maps pages and see if you can identify the picture clues below.

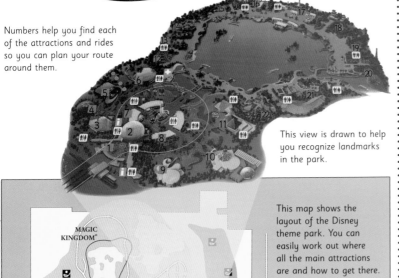

Numbers help you find each of the attractions and rides so you can plan your route around them.

This view is drawn to help you recognize landmarks in the park.

This map shows the layout of the Disney theme park. You can easily work out where all the main attractions are and how to get there.

MAGIC KINGDOM

Ticket and Transportation Center

ORLANDO

Downtown Disney

Exit 68

EPCOT

DISNEY'S ANIMAL KINGDOM

Blizzard Beach

Winter Summerland

DISNEY'S HOLLYWOOD STUDIOS

Typhoon Lagoon

536

Exit 67

Orlando International Airport

4

TAMPA

IRLO BRONSON MEMORIAL HIGHWAY

Disney's Wide World of Sports

192

Exit 64B

KISSIMMEE

TAMPA

Become an expert...

on using a map, pages 106-107

on types of map, pages 114-115

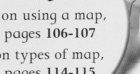

A cartographer.

Early maps

Maps have changed a lot since the first ones appeared, when those drawing a map would often use their imagination to fill in unknown areas.

This re-creation of Ptolemy's map from **The Geography** dates back to 1540.

Early mapmakers often chose to fill empty spaces with imaginary beasts.

1,900 years ago

A geographer called Ptolemy (c. 100–c. 170) wrote *The Geography*, which included a world map and looked at what was known about mapping. The maps were lost, but copies appeared in the 1500s based on Ptolemy's coordinates.

2000 BCE

500 BCE

100 CE

4,000 to 3,500 years ago

Valcamonica in north Italy is home to the most ancient maps known in Europe, including the Bedolina Map. Drawn on rock, it shows fields with crops, animals, houses, and paths.

Imago Mundi

2,500 years ago

The Babylonian *Imago Mundi* was a clay tablet and showed Babylon at the centre of the world. Early mapmakers often centred a map on their country in this way.

2,200 years ago

A Greek mathematician called Eratosthenes (c. 276–194 BCE) made the first-known calculation about Earth's circumference. It's thought he was wrong by just one per cent!

Eratosthenes's work helped to turn geography and map making into a recognized science.

What is geography?

The Carta Marina is a sea map drawn in the 1500s.

Rosselli's map measured just 15 x 28 cm (6 x 11 in).

800 years ago

In the 1200s, a monk made a copy of a map from the late Roman Empire. Known as the *Tabula Peutingeriana*, it is almost 6.8 metres (22 ft) long, but just 34 cm (13 in) wide and is basically a road map.

500 years ago

In 1508, Italian painter Cosimo Rosselli produced an amazingly detailed, but tiny world map. He even showed the undiscovered Antarctica.

1200

1500

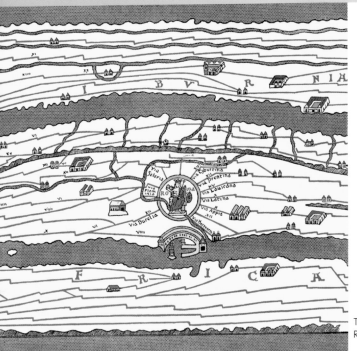

600 years ago

The Danish geographer Claudius Clausson Swart drew the first known map of Northern Europe in 1427.

The **Tabula Peutingeriana** shows Roman roads from Spain to India.

105

Using a map

If you go for a walk around somewhere you don't know, you'll find it easier if you know how to use a map. Not only does a map stop you getting lost, but the right map tells you exactly where the footpaths, shortcuts, and good views are.

Arc de Triomphe, Paris, France

The direct or scenic route
A map helps you to plan how you would like to get from one place to another. Why not see the sights?

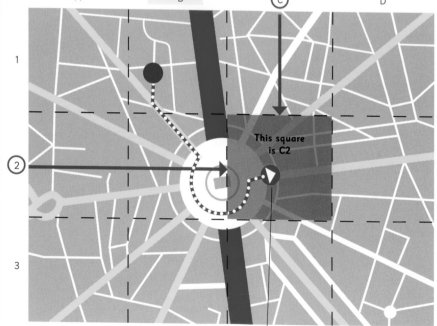

This street map of Paris is divided into a grid of squares. The driver's route was from a place in B1 to a place in C2.

This square is C2

Using a grid

How do you find something on a map? You use a grid reference. Printed maps have letters and numbers around the edge of the map, which help you to find a location. An index entry may direct you to 106 C2. 106 is the page number. You then follow across to column C and down to row 2.

Where is magnetic north?

Take a compass

A compass is helpful when reading a map as it tells you which way is north. Even in thick fog, a compass can help you find out which way to go.

Be prepared! Take a compass with you on a countryside walk.

A compass has four main points: north, south, east, and west.

Hands on

Magnetize a needle by stroking a magnet 50 times along it, away from the point. Put the needle on some cork and float on water. The needle will point north.

How to use a compass

Turn yourself and your compass until the red arrow is facing north. Place it on the map in the same direction as the magnetic north arrow shown on your map. Pick out a feature on the map in the landscape in front of you.

That's too high to climb!

Countryside maps are usually shaded to show different levels in the ground, as well as physical features you will find. Contour lines are lines that connect points of equal height. The difference between two contour lines that are next to each other may be up to 300 m (1,000 ft).

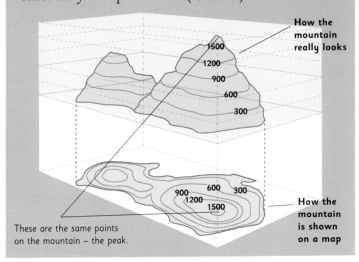

How the mountain really looks

1500
1200
900
600
300

How the mountain is shown on a map

900 600 300
1200
1500

These are the same points on the mountain – the peak.

Legend

▬▬▬	Trunk road
▭▭▭	Main road
▭▭▭	Secondary road
▭▬▭	Railway
〰️	Stream
▬	Park

Airport
Camping
View
Shops
Toilets
Telephone
Bus stop

What does that mean?

Mapmakers use symbols to represent a map's major features. The symbols save space, meaning more information can be included on the map. The symbols are listed in a key, or "legend". Symbols usually look a bit like the things they represent.

Somewhere in the Arctic but it keeps moving.

Not just a line!

Large-scale maps have lines forming a grid over the country or countries shown. These are lines of latitude and longitude, and they are there because they make it easy to pinpoint a place anywhere in the world.

This diagram shows how lines of latitude slice Earth into imaginary horizontal sections.

This diagram shows how lines of longitude split Earth into imaginary segments.

Cutting the globe in half

The equator is the imaginary line, shown below in red, that cuts the world in half. It is the longest latitude line going around the world. At the equator, the latitude is zero degrees.

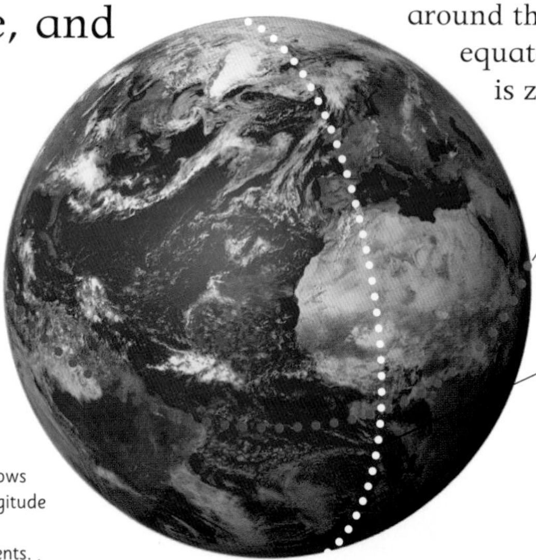

The equator

Eight countries lie on the Prime Meridian: United Kingdom, France, Spain, Algeria, Mali, Burkina Faso, Ghana, and Togo.

The Prime Meridian

This is the point at which the lines of longitude are at zero degrees. It was fixed at a point in Greenwich, England, in 1884 after a conference in America, because different systems were making shipping and trade difficult.

What is latitude?

The lines that run straight across a map tell you how far north or south you are from the equator. If you were near the North Pole, you would be at 90 degrees north. If you were near the South Pole, you would be at 90 degrees south.

What is longitude?

The lines that run straight up a map tell you where you are east or west of the Greenwich Prime Meridian. You can be up to 180 degrees east or west of this imaginary line.

A selection of cities are marked onto the ground at the Prime Meridian in Greenwich.

What latitude is halfway between the equator and the North Pole?

Putting it all together

If you know the latitude and longitude of a city, you can easily find it on a world map or globe.

East of the Prime Meridian, the time advances an hour for every 15 degrees of longitude. Go west and you lose an hour every 15 degrees. Greenwich is about five hours ahead of New York.

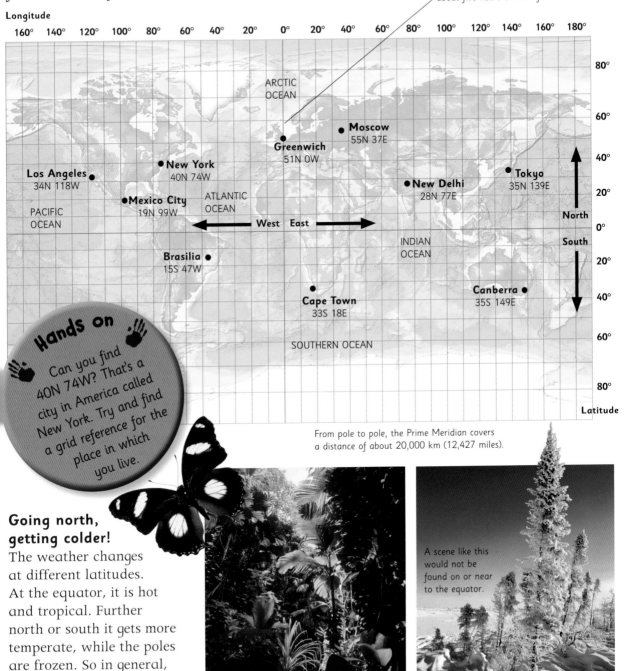

Longitude

160° 140° 120° 100° 80° 60° 40° 20° 0° 20° 40° 60° 80° 100° 120° 140° 160° 180°

ARCTIC OCEAN

Moscow
55N 37E

Greenwich
51N 0W

New York
40N 74W

Los Angeles
34N 118W

Tokyo
35N 139E

New Delhi
28N 77E

Mexico City
19N 99W

ATLANTIC
OCEAN

PACIFIC
OCEAN

West   East

North

South

INDIAN
OCEAN

Brasilia
15S 47W

Canberra
35S 149E

Cape Town
33S 18E

SOUTHERN OCEAN

80° 60° 40° 20° 0° 20° 40° 60° 80°

Latitude

Hands on

Can you find 40N 74W? That's a city in America called New York. Try and find a grid reference for the place in which you live.

From pole to pole, the Prime Meridian covers a distance of about 20,000 km (12,427 miles).

Going north, getting colder!

The weather changes at different latitudes. At the equator, it is hot and tropical. Further north or south it gets more temperate, while the poles are frozen. So in general, the further you are from the equator, the cooler the air temperature.

Tropical rainforests lie around the equator.

A scene like this would not be found on or near to the equator.

Mapping the world

World maps distort what you see, because although maps can reflect some features accurately, they are printed on a flat surface and the Earth is spherical. That means sizes and shapes have to shift around a little.

Making the globe flat

Have you ever given a football as a present? Did you find it hard to wrap? Similarly, it's hard to turn Earth into a flat map. Mapmakers do it by projection. There are more than 200 kinds of map projection.

Projection

Three main types of map projection are used.

Conic projection
Conic projection is often used to map the poles. Imagine a cone of paper held over a globe.

Cylindrical
Cylindrical projection is made up from a tube or cylinder of paper being wrapped around the globe.

Azimuthal
For this, a flat sheet of paper is held at one point, and a map made of that portion of the globe.

Mercator's projection

This is the most familiar of projections and first appeared in 1569. However, it makes Greenland look larger than it is.

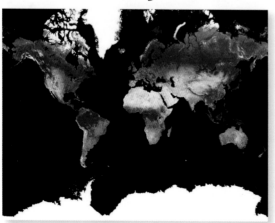

Mercator's map was taken from a cylindrical projection of Earth.

Gall-Peters' projection

In 1973, Arno Peters published this map based on a projection by James Gall in 1855. It gives a better representation of the true areas of Earth's continents.

The Gall-Peters' map is well known, but has not been adopted widely as a world map.

Who was Ptolemy?

Shifting the centre

Looking at maps in a different way provides a completely different view of the world. In Japan and China, world maps are sold with the Pacific Ocean as the centre.

A map centred on the Pacific Ocean shows how large this ocean really is.

Become an expert...

on early maps, pages 104-105;

on making maps, pages 112-113

Europe

Asia

Africa

North America

Atlantic Ocean

Australasia

South America

An upside-down world

There is no reason for maps to always have north at the top – this is simply because that's how Ptolemy (who lived between 100 and 170 CE) drew his world map. Stuart McArthur is an Australian who wanted to see his country at the top of a map.

McArthur's world map was first published in 1979.

MCARTHUR'S UNIVERSAL CORRECTIVE MAP OF THE WORLD

He was a geographer (and mathematician). Learn more on page 104.

Making maps

Maps were once hand drawn and illustrated, a process that could take a year. Nowadays, computer data banks hold so much geographical information, it takes only minutes to create a detailed map.

This map shows some of the landscape (pink) and archaeological (red) features found in Caffarella Park, Rome, Italy.

Mapping by satellite

Satellites take photographs of a country in sections and send these images to mapping stations on Earth, which link them together and translate them into maps. They also use radar to measure land heights accurately.

Solar panels provide power

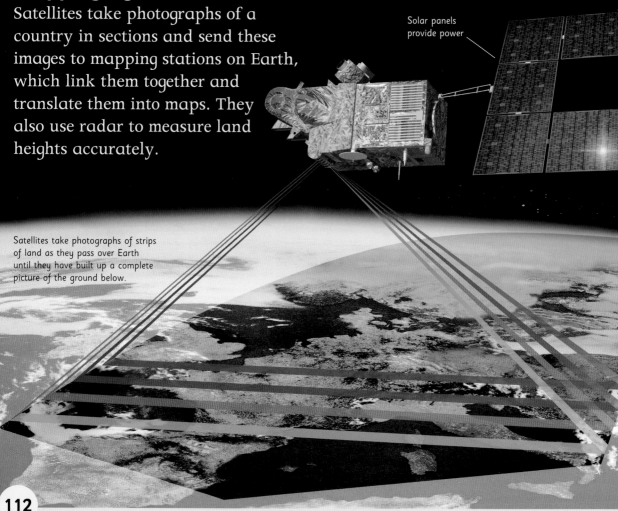

Satellites take photographs of strips of land as they pass over Earth until they have built up a complete picture of the ground below.

What is topography?

Surveyors measure heights and distances with theodolites.

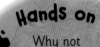

Mapping on the ground

Smaller maps are still made using traditional methods. When new areas of parkland, for example, are designed, a landscape architect or surveyor will visit the site and map the area by taking measurements. These are used to draw precise maps.

Gridded paper is useful for scale drawings.

Hands on

Why not make your own map – it could be a plan of your street and home, or map of a local park. Plan your drawing from a bird's-eye (overhead) view.

A mission to map the world

In just 11 days in 2000, the space shuttle *Endeavour* used radar to collect detailed measurements of 80 per cent of Earth's land mass. It gave valuable information for 3-D map making.

Endeavour's mission is known as the Shuttle Radar Topography Mission, or SRTM.

It's all in the detail

The maps produced as a result of *Endeavour's* mission are incredibly detailed, showing the exact height of mountain ranges and depth of valleys.

This 3-D map of Mount St Helens, USA, shows how it looks in the landscape.

Undersea maps

Ships use echo sounders to send waves down to the sea bed. The waves bounce back when they hit the bottom, and the time they take indicates the depth. On a sea chart, dark blue means deep water. Light blue shows shallow water. Ocean maps are also created by satellites.

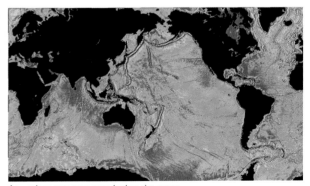

An underwater map reveals that the ocean basins are not as flat as you might think.

It is the physical shape of the features in a landscape.

Types of map

Road maps, town street maps, transport maps, sailing charts, star charts, political maps… there are endless varieties of maps.

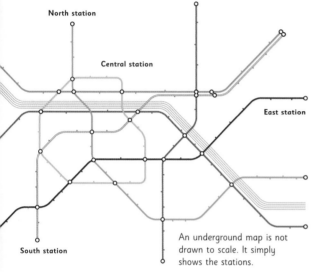

An underground map is not drawn to scale. It simply shows the stations.

Let's look at the route!

Road maps are widely used. They cover a larger area than a street map, and use different colours and lines to represent different roads. On most road maps, motorways are blue.

A selection of road maps

Let's walk that way

Street maps are often provided free at major train terminals. They are helpful for people who don't know the local area. They include major landmarks.

I'll pick up a tube map

Maps that show transport networks, such as bus routes or underground lines, have to be easy to read. They don't need to reflect accurate distances, but they do need to show the order of stops or stations on the route.

Lost? Check the map.

What type of map does not show accurate distances?

Physical map

This type of map identifies the main geographical features, such as mountains, lakes, rivers, deserts, forests, and oceans.

Political map

If you want to learn a bit about the world's countries, look at a political map. These show national and state borders, while different countries are provided with different colours.

Europe has many countries.

On the move

You can now look up maps on a computer screen or mobile phone, making it easy for walkers and car drivers to find destinations.

Computer maps

Around the world, specially fitted bicycles and cars have taken images that have been uploaded to provide extensive views of the places we live.

Easy internet connections mean mobile phone users can easily plan their route.

This bicycle is taking photographs to be used on Google Earth.

Bus, train, and underground maps.

Map of the world

If you flatten out our world, this is what it looks like. There is very little land and a lot of water. Most of the land sits north of the equator. At the top and bottom of our planet are two icy polar regions.

Greenland

Canada

North America

Atlantic Ocean

Pacific Ocean

South America

Continents and oceans

There are seven main land masses that form our continents: North and South America, Africa, Europe, Asia, Australasia, and Antarctica. These are surrounded by five major oceans: the Pacific, the Atlantic, the Indian, the Arctic, and the Southern Oceans.

Become an expert...

on map projections, pages 110-111
on making maps, pages 112-113

Antarctica

Which is the largest of the five oceans?

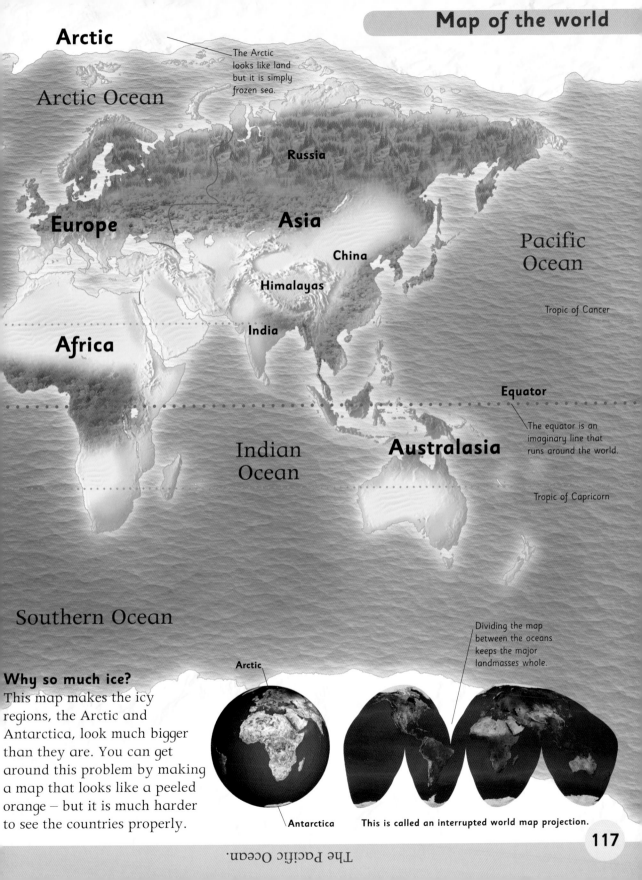

Arctic

The Arctic looks like land but it is simply frozen sea.

Arctic Ocean

Russia

Europe

Asia

China

Himalayas

India

Pacific Ocean

Tropic of Cancer

Africa

Equator

The equator is an imaginary line that runs around the world.

Indian Ocean

Australasia

Tropic of Capricorn

Southern Ocean

Dividing the map between the oceans keeps the major landmasses whole.

Why so much ice?

This map makes the icy regions, the Arctic and Antarctica, look much bigger than they are. You can get around this problem by making a map that looks like a peeled orange – but it is much harder to see the countries properly.

Arctic

Antarctica

This is called an interrupted world map projection.

Picture this!

We've visited some remarkable places in this book, but our planet is full of natural wonders. Here are some other amazing locations that we didn't want to you to miss.

The Grand Prismatic Spring in Yellowstone Park, USA, is really colourful because of the minerals dissolved in its hot waters.

The highest waterfall in the world is the Angel Falls in Venezuela.

The Moon rises over the strange landscape of Monument Valley, USA.

The waters of Milford Sound, New Zealand, are surrounded by steep cliffs that were carved out by glaciers.

Do you know what Uluru used to be called?

Uluru is a giant lump of sandstone rock right in the middle of Australia.

The Antarctic can look very blue when you're out on the ice field.

The Remarkable Rocks on Kangaroo Island, Australia, have been shaped by the wind and rain.

The Zambezi River drops into a huge crack in the ground at the Victoria Falls in Africa.

Mount Fuji in Japan is claimed to be the most perfectly shaped volcano on Earth.

Ayer's Rock.

The world at night

Did you know that the lights in our homes, schools, and offices can be seen from space? It's clear where the world's major cities are when you look at this world map.

The east coast of the USA is so lit up you can see the outlines of the Great Lakes to the northwest.

Atlantic Ocean

Flying down to Rio? Even if you go at night it isn't hard to find.

Vancouver, Canada

It is the light pouring out from billions of street and office lights that makes cities such as Vancouver visible from space at night.

Kept in the dark

There are still a few dark places left in the world. These are mainly areas that have a poor electricity supply or a small population, such as deserts, rainforests, and mountain ranges.

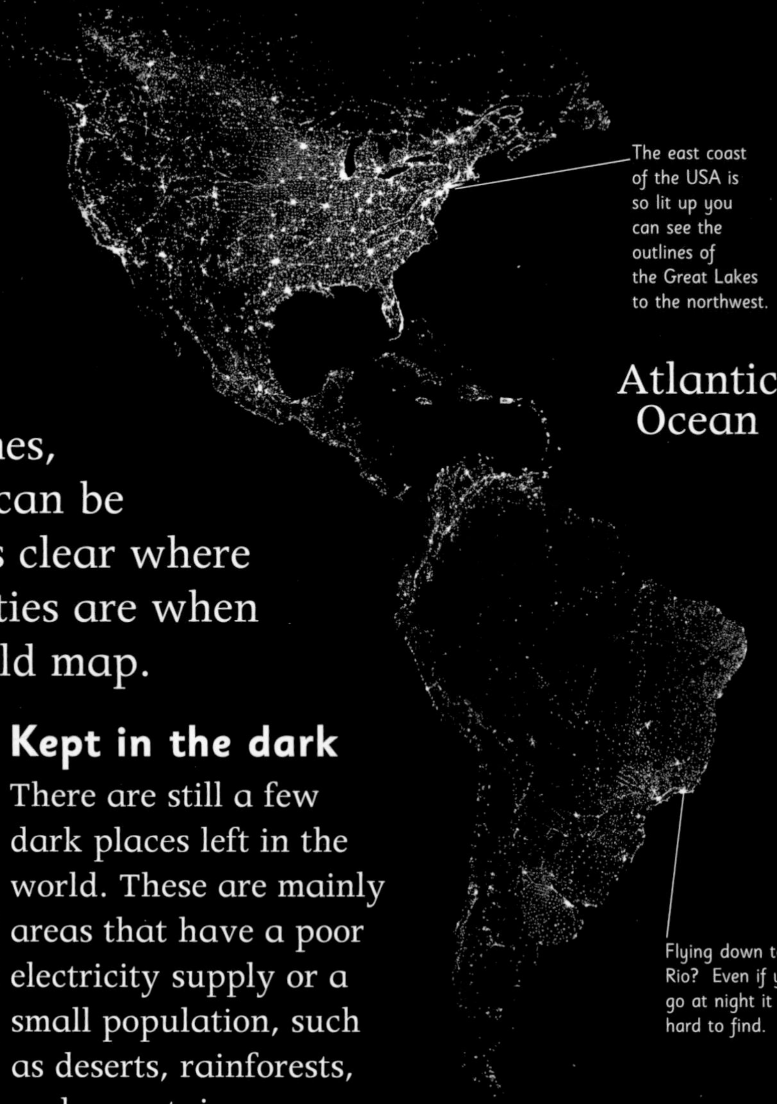

Do you know what country Tokyo is in?

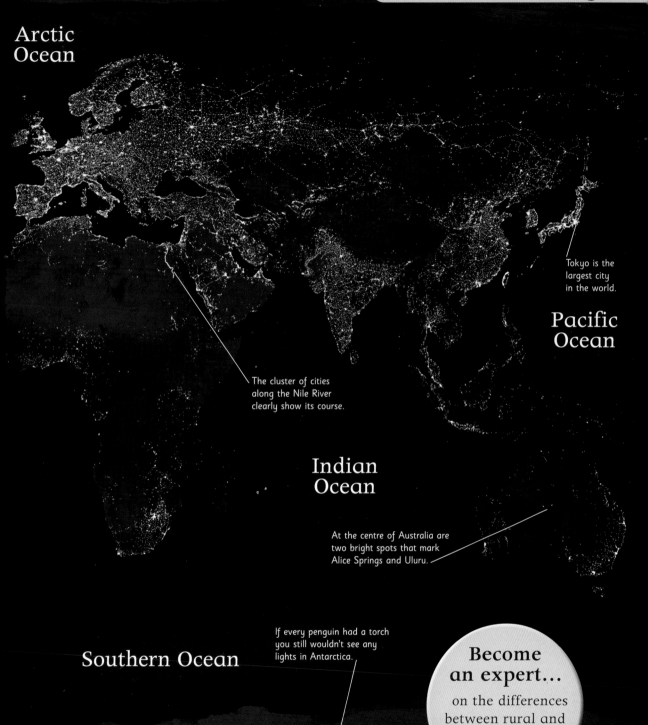

Arctic Ocean

Tokyo is the largest city in the world.

Pacific Ocean

The cluster of cities along the Nile River clearly show its course.

Indian Ocean

At the centre of Australia are two bright spots that mark Alice Springs and Uluru.

If every penguin had a torch you still wouldn't see any lights in Antarctica.

Southern Ocean

Become an expert...

on the differences between rural and urban areas, pages 72-73

Glossary

atmosphere The mass of air that surrounds Earth.

atoll A ring of coral reef surrounding a lagoon.

biome Any of Earth's major ecosystems with a particular climate and vegetation.

climate The average weather conditions over a period of time.

continent A large area of land visible above the ocean.

coordinates A system where numbers and/or letters are used to find a location on a map.

coral Colonies of tiny animals that live in the sea. They form a hard outer covering to protect their soft bodies. These gradually build up into huge stony reefs.

crust The thin layer of surface rock that makes up the continents and ocean floor.

culture The shared beliefs and views of a group of people. It can also include the traditions, art, food, music, and other creative talents of those people.

current The movement of water or air in a particular direction.

ecosystem The community of animals and plants living in a particular area.

environment The surroundings of a living thing or an object.

equator An imaginary line that runs horizontally around Earth.

erosion The breaking down of rock by water or the weather.

fossil fuel Fuels formed from the remains of animals and plants that lived millions of years ago. They include oil and coal.

glacier A large mass of ice that moves slowly down a slope.

gravity A force that pulls everything towards Earth's centre.

greenhouse gases Gases in Earth's atmosphere that trap heat from the Sun and warm the planet.

industry The production of goods for use and sale.

landmark A feature of the landscape that is easy to recognize, such as the Eiffel Tower in Paris, or an oddly shaped rock.

limestone A soft sedimentary rock that is often made from broken shells.

magma Molten rock flowing beneath Earth's surface. When it flows onto the surface it is called lava.

magnetic north The direction that a compass needle points on Earth, except at the exact North Pole, where it points due south.

mantle A thick layer of rock between Earth's crust and its core.

microorganism A tiny creature that can only be seen with a microscope.

mineral A solid chemical substance usually found as crystals in rock.

Which direction does a compass point if you're standing at the North Pole?

nutrients Chemicals that plants and animals need to make them grow.

ozone A colourless gas that forms a layer in the atmosphere. It helps absorb most of the harmful rays in sunlight.

photosynthesis The process by which plants make their own food using energy from the Sun.

plankton Tiny animals (zooplankton) and plants (phytoplankton) that live in the sunlit upper layer of water.

polar region An area of land or sea around the North or South Poles.

pollution Waste substances that have been dumped into the air, water, or on land. They can often have a harmful effect on the environment.

population The number of living things in an area. You can have populations of animals and plants, as well as humans.

porous Any material that has spaces between it that lets water flow through. Soil is porous.

predator An animal that hunts and eats other animals.

projection The name given to any type of map that shows the spherical Earth on a flat sheet.

radar A device that uses radio waves to detect moving or fixed objects. It works by bouncing a wave off the object and timing how long it takes to come back. You can then calculate the distance.

reef A rocky structure that lies beneath the surface of the ocean.

resort Any place used for relaxation and recreation.

satellite A spacecraft that orbits Earth. They are used for monitoring events on Earth, such as the weather and volcanic eruptions, and for measuring Earth's surface.

sediment Tiny, broken-down pieces of rock carried by rivers and glaciers.

seismograph A machine that measures the shaking of an earthquake.

surveyor Somebody who measures land distances and heights.

suspension bridge Type of bridge where the deck is supported by cables that are hung from upright towers.

tectonics The movement of the giant rocky plates that make up Earth's crust.

theodolite An instrument used by a surveyor to measure heights and distances.

topography The study of Earth's surface shape and features.

tundra A cold, treeless region near the poles where the soil remains frozen for most of the year.

water vapour The gaseous form of water in the atmosphere. You can see it as clouds or mist.

To the South Pole.

Index

Reference section

M
Madagascar 49
magma 16
magnetic north 122
malaria 85
Mandarin Chinese 86, 87
mantle 8, 9, 11, 122
manufacturing 93
mapmakers 107, 112-113
maps 102-115
marine iguana 23
markets 94
McArthur, Stuart 111
Mercator 110
Mesosaurus 10
mesosphere 12
metamorphic 14
meteors 13
microclimate 35
Mid-autumn festival 101
Milford Sound 118
minerals 15, 28, 53, 68, 88, 122
mining 68, 92
Monument Valley 118
Moon 45
mosquitoes 85
mountains 20-21, 35, 47, 70
Mount Everest 20
Mount Fuji 119
Mount Pinatubo 17
Mount St Helens 11, 113
Mount Vesuvius 83

N
Nile River 121
North America 89, 90
nutrients 66, 123

O
oases 61
oceans 64-65
Okavango Delta 63
oxygen 12, 13, 42, 56
ozone 13, 123

P
Pacific Garbage Patch 97
Pacific Ocean 19, 28, 39, 64, 65, 97
palm trees 61
pampas 58, 59
Pangaea 10
Pantanal 62-63
Passover 100
penguins 51
people 55, 68, 84-85, 88
permafrost 53
petrol 93
Philippines 87
photosynthesis 56
phytoplankton 65
pipes 53
plankton 65
plants 12, 25, 41, 49, 52, 61, 65
plastics 97
plates (Earth's) 10, 11
polar bear 50
political map 115
pollution 40-41, 95, 123
Pompeii 83
population 74, 84-85

prairies 58, 59
precipitation 29
Prime Meridian 108
projection 110
Ptolemy 104, 111
pyramids 80
Pyrenees 70

Q
quadrat 48

R
rain 37
rainbows 37
rainforests 7, 46, 48, 56-57, 109
rain gauge 37
recycling 41, 97
reindeer 53
Remarkable Rocks 119
reservoirs 28, 29, 82
resources 88-89, 94-95
Rhine River 71
rice 63, 92
ring of fire 19
Rio de Janeiro 74
rivers 7, 14, 27, 30-31, 71
road maps 114
rocks 9, 14, 15
Rosselli, Cosimo 105
rubbish 96-97
runoff 29
rural 72-73
Russia 87

Picture credits

The publisher would like to thank the following for their kind permission to reproduce their photographs:

(Key: a-above; b-below/bottom; c-centre; f-far; l-left; r-right; t-top)

1 Corbis: Ken Davies / Flame (cla). **Getty Images:** Hiroyuki Matsumoto / Photographer's Choice (main image); Robert Harding World Imagery (clb). **2 Planetary Visions Limited:** (tr). **2-3 Corbis:** Yann Arthus-Bertrand. **4 Getty Images:** NASA (fbr/satellite image). **NASA:** (cra/satellite image). **Science Photo Library:** Jim Reed (tr); Irene Windridge (br/fire). **5 Alamy Images:** The Art Gallery Collection (tc); Mark & Audrey Gibson / Stock Connection Blue (clb/cartographer). **Corbis:** Rudy Sulgan (br). **Getty Images:** Frans Lemmens / Photographer's Choice (cb). **iStockphoto.com:** Iconeer (t/map background). **Photolibrary:** North Wind Picture Archives (tl). **Science Photo Library:** Anakaopress / Look At Sciences (bl/volcanologists); British Antarctic Survey (clb/geologists); Mark C. Burnett (clb/town planner); Alexis Rosenfeld (clb/ecologists); Science Source (tr). **6-7 Corbis:** Walter Geiersperger (main image). **7 Corbis:** Richard Ashworth / Robert Harding World Imagery (crb); Tom Bean (cra); Bettmann (tr); Don Hammond / Design Pics (crb/lava); Neil Rabinowitz (cr); Keren Su (br). **9 Corbis:** Don Hammond / Design Pics (crb). **Dorling Kindersley:** Natural History Museum, London (cra/granite). **10 Corbis:** Fotofeeling / Westend61 (cl). **10-11 Corbis:** Geoff Renner / Robert Harding World Imagery (b). **11 Getty Images:** InterNetwork Media / Photodisc (br). **12 Alamy Images:** Arterra Picture Library (cla). **Corbis:** Bryan Allen (clb/mesosphere). **Getty Images:** Runstudio (bl) (clb/balloon). **Science Photo Library:** NASA (tl). **12-13 Corbis:** NASA (earth view) (cra). **13 Corbis:** Bryan Allen (br). **NASA:** GSFC (bl). **14 Dorling Kindersley:** Natural History Museum, London (cra/sedimentary rock). **15 Alamy Images:** Nick Greaves (r/mountain & sky) (tc/feldspar) (tr/granite) (tr/mica). **Dorling Kindersley:** Natural History Museum, London (tl/quartz) (ca) (cla). **iStockphoto.com:** Tom Brown (fbr); Craftvision (crb); Fernando Delvalle (clb/bicycle); Luca di Filippo (br/laptop) (bl/can) (cb/bricks); DNY59 (crb/backpack & books); Floortje (clb/flip flops); Taylor Hinton (clb/house); Rafa Irusta (crb/hair dryer); Jitalia17 (clb/mug); Jsemeniuk (clb/digital camera); Alexander Kalina (bc/trainers); Kledge (bl/American football); KRUS (bl/paint & brush); Eduardo Leite (bl/wristwatch); Mammamaart (bc/beach ball); Pagadesign (crb/car); Martin Pernter (crb/goggles); Vadim Ponomarenko (crb/jewellery). **16 Corbis:** Frans Lanting (l); Visuals Unlimited (br). **17 Corbis:** Yann Arthus-Bertrand (b); Bettmann (cr); Roger Ressmeyer (cl) (cra/rope-shaped rock). **Dorling Kindersley:** Natural History Museum, London (tr/chunk). **Science Photo Library:** Robert M. Carey, NOAA (tl). **18 Corbis:** Tom Bean (bl). **Science Photo Library:** Gary Hincks (cr); Zephyr (tl). **19 Corbis:** Guo Jian She / Redlink (br). **Science Photo Library:** Gary Hincks (cl). **20 Alamy Images:** Westend 61 GmbH (tl). **Corbis:** Ray Juno (clb/cabin); Galen Rowell (main image). **iStockphoto.com:** Andy Gehrig (cl/leopard); Charles Schug (cla/trees). **22 Corbis:** Richard T. Nowitz (crb); Douglas Peebles (tr); Keren Su (b). **23 Getty Images:** Bobby Model / National Geographic (tl). **Science Photo Library:** Steve Allen (bc); Planetobserver (clb). **24 Corbis:** Arctic-Images (crb). **Getty Images:** Popperfoto (clb). **Photoshot:** Stella Snead (bl). **Science Photo Library:** Worldsat International (tr). **24-25 Alamy Images:** Arctic Images / Ragnar Th Sigurdsson. **25 Corbis:** Bob Krist (bc); Arthur Morris (cla). **26 Alamy Images:** geographyphotos (tr). **Corbis:** Thomas Schulze / EPA (b). **27 Corbis:** Peter Adams (br); Momatiuk - Eastcott (tr); Jim Wark / Visuals Unlimited (tl). **28 Corbis:** Richard Ashworth / Robert Harding World Imagery (bl); Pascal Parrot / Sygma (ca). **Getty Images:** Philippe Roy / hemis.fr (crb). **Science Photo Library:** Planetary Visions Ltd (tl). **29 Getty Images:** Leonardo Papini / SambaPhoto (crb). **30 Corbis:** Gary Braasch (bc); Neil Rabinowitz (cr). **www.airphotona.com:** Jim Wark (l). **31 Alamy Images:** Horizon International Images Limited (bc/city). **Corbis:** Philip Wallick (cr). **Courtesy of the National Science Foundation:** Zina Deretsky / NSF (cl). **32 Alamy Images:** Ladi Kirn (bl/proteus anguinus). **Ardea:** Pat Morris (clb/salamander). **Corbis:** Arne Hodalic (clb/cave fish). **Dorling Kindersley:** Natural History Museum, London (bl/spider). **Getty Images:** Hans Strand (background) (bc). **33 Corbis:** Bertrand Gardel (tr); M. L. Sinibaldi (ca). **fotoLibra :** Miles Kelly (tl). **National Geographic Stock:** Carsten Peter / Speleoresearch & Films (b). **34 Corbis:** Dan Brownsword (l/frozen landscape); Blaine Harrington III (cla). **Getty Images:** Stuart Dee / Photographer's Choice (fcla). **35 Corbis:** Jacques Langevin / Sygma (bc); Radius Images (r/desert landscape); Craig Tuttle (tr). **Getty Images:** Harald Sund (cra). **36 Corbis:** Chuck Doswell / VisualsUnlimited (r/tornado). **Science Photo Library:** NASA (bl). **37 Corbis:** Meijert de Haan / EPA (cr/waterspout); Mark A. Johnson (ca/rainbow); Larry Mulvehill (tr/tree); Jim Reed (cra/thunderstorm) (cl); Ariel Skelley / BlendImages (cra/girl); Tetra Images (cra/snowman). **Getty Images:** Jean-Pierre Pieuchot (crb/fog). **Science Photo Library:** Cape Grim B.A.P.S. / Simon Fraser (bl); Michael Donne (fbr); European Space Agency / Aeos Medialab (br); U.S. Air Force (fbl/plane). **38 Corbis:** Kazuyoshi Nomachi (tr). **Getty Images:** artpartner-images / Photographer's Choice (l/desert background). **iStockphoto.com:** Bill Bartholomew (cb/car). **39 Getty Images:** Michael Fogden / Photolibrary (tr); Marko Georgiev (b); Ronaldo Schemidt / AFP (cla) (br/city background). **40 Corbis:** Imagemore Co., Ltd (cr); Kulka / zefa (tr/earth). **Getty Images:** Cultura / Steve Sparrow (br); Kazuo Ogawa / amana images (cl). **Science Photo Library:** David R. Frazier (bl). **41 Corbis:** Alan Schein Photography (cr); Bettmann (cl); Simon Jarratt (cra/boy); Radius Images (cra/recycling symbol). **Getty Images:** Mike Brinson (br); JGI / Jamie Grill / Blend Images (cra/switch); Ben Osborne (bl); STOCK4B-RF (tr). **Science Photo Library:** Chris Knapton (tl). **42 Corbis:** amanaimages (br/grass); Ken Davies / Flame (tree in field); Matthias Kulka (cra/iceberg) (br); Don Smith / Robert Harding World Imagery (bl/x).

Getty Images: Don Mason (cr) (crb/wheat) (crb). **NASA:** Lick Observatory (cra/moon); Hans Eggensberger / fStop (tc/x) (cla/x). **44 Getty Images:** NASA (t). **NASA:** (bl). **44-45 Corbis:** Kulka / zefa (cb/earth). **45 Getty Images:** Wolfgang Kaehler (cr). **NASA:** Cassini Imaging Team / Cassini Project (br) (bl). **46 Corbis:** Tim McGuire (tr). **Getty Images:** P. Jaccod / De Agostini (br); Alejandra Parra / Bloomberg (bl/parrot); Karim Sahib / AFP (cla); Gordon Wiltsie / National Geographic (bl/forest background behind parrot). **47 Getty Images:** Theo Heimann / AFP (br); Steven Kazlowski / Barcroft Media (tr); Tauseef Mustafa / AFP (cra); Fabio Muzzi / AFP (bl); Franc & Jean Shor / National Geographic (tl). **48 Alamy Images:** Chris Howes / Wild Places Photography (bl). **iStockphoto.com:** Craftvision (cra/turf). **naturepl.com:** Kim Taylor (c). **49 Corbis:** Martin Harvey / Gallo Images (l). **FLPA:** Ingo Arndt / Minden Pictures (ca). **Photolibrary:** Iconotec (tr). **Science Photo Library:** Planetobserver (tc); © 1995, Worldsat International & J. Knighton (br). **50 Corbis:** DLILLC (br/walrus); Matthias Kulka (bl); Kennan Ward (cra). **Getty Images:** Ralph Lee Hopkins / National Geographic (cl); Roy Toft (br/seal). **SeaPics.com:** John K. B. Ford / Ursus (crb/narwhal). **51 Corbis:** DLILLC (cra/penguin); Kevin Schafer (b); Norbert Wu / Science Faction (cr/starfish). **Getty Images:** Sue Flood (crahumpback); Nathalie Michel (cra/orca). **Science Photo Library:** British Antarctic Survey (cla). **52 Alamy Images:** Wayne Lynch / All Canada Photos (bc). **Getty Images:** Olivier Grunewald / Photolibrary (fbl); Michael Melford / National Geographic (tr). **52-53 Bryan & Cherry Alexander / ArcticPhoto:** T. Jacobsen (main image). **53 Alamy Images:** Bryan and Cherry Alexander / Arcticphoto (tl); Wayne Lynch / All Canada Photos (cr). **Bryan & Cherry Alexander / ArcticPhoto:** (bl); T. Jacobsen (br). **Getty Images:** Cary Anderson / Aurora (tr); Tom Murphy / National Geographic (cra/Arctic fox); Paul Nicklen / National Geographic (cra/lemming); Paul Oomen / Photographer's Choice (cra/musk ox); Joel Sartore / National Geographic (ca) (crb). **54 Getty Images:** Nacivet (fbr); Jessica Ojala / Flickr (l/forest); Greg Probst (cr/coniferous). **54-55 Getty Images:** Peter Haigh (background trees); pasmal / amanaimagesRF (t/leaves). **Getty Images:** Tim Flach (clb/ants); Huntstock (cra); Lester Lefkowitz (c/forklift) (tc). **56 Corbis:** Frans Lanting (bl) (cb/parakeets). **Getty Images:** Giles Breton / Flickr (br/parakeets flying). **56-57 Alamy Images:** Images & Stories (b/forest). **57 Corbis:** Frans Lanting (bl). **Getty Images:** James Balog / The Image Bank (cra/ jaguar); Giles Breton / Flickr (br/parakeets); Daniel J. Cox (cra/orangutans); Leo Freitas / Flickr (clb); Martin Harvey / Gallo Images (crb/okapi); Gavriel Jecan / Photographer's Choice (cra/toucan); Mattias Klum / National Geographic (crb/butterfly); Roy Toft / National Geographic (cr/frog). **58 Getty Images:** Annie Griffiths Belt (bl) (tl). **Science Photo Library:** Jon Van De Grift / Visuals Unlimited (br). **58-59 Getty Images:** Panoramic Images (cb/grassland background). **59 Ecolibrary.org:** Dan L. Perlman (bl); Jason Edwards / National Geographic (cr/red oat grass). **Getty Images:** Jason Edwards / National Geographic (cra/spinifex); Tim Graham (tr/barley); Mark Harmel (cra/foxtail); Adam Jones (tl); Diego Uchitel (tc). **60 Corbis:** Destinations (cla). **Getty Images:** Simon Weller (cl). **Photolibrary:** Glow Images, Inc. (ca). **SuperStock:** Photononstop (bl). **60-61 SuperStock:** age fotostock (background). **61 Alamy Images:** imagebroker (cr/palm trees). **Corbis:** Liu Liqun (br). **Getty Images:** Nico Tondini (tr); Bert and Babs Wells (crb/thorny devil). **Photolibrary:** Mike Hill (crb/jerboa). **62 Getty Images:** Theo Allofs (cra/swamp); Nat Photos (c/floodlands); Nancy Nehring (cr/capybara); Travel Ink (cra/marsh); Darwin Wiggett (cra/shallows); Win Initiative (cra/bog) (bl). **Planetary Visions Limited:** (cla/globe). **62-63 Getty Images:** Nat Photos (b/water lillies). **63 Getty Images:** Jeremy Frechette (crb); Martin Harvey (tl); Beverly Joubert / National Geographic (c); marin.tomic / Flickr (tr); Laurie Rubin (cra/rice sprig); Chris Stein (cr/rice grains) (c/sunlit). **64 Getty Images:** Barcroft Media (clb/whale); Daniel Cooper (cra); Peter David (bl). **65 Corbis:** Tobias Bernhard (cl/herring); Stephen Frink (tc); Image Source (background); Amos Nachoum (ca/killer whale); Hein van den Heuvel (bl). **Getty Images:** Stephen Frink (cla/sea lion). **Science Photo Library:** Steve Gschmeissner (crb/phytoplankton); NASA / GSFC (bc); Michael Patrick O'neill (c/lemonfish); Wim Van Egmond / Visuals Unlimited (cb/zooplankton). **66 iStockphoto.com:** Craftvision (cb/grass). **naturepl.com:** Meul / ARCO (b/earthworms). **67 Corbis:** AgStock Image (br). **Dorling Kindersley:** Stephen Oliver (bl/3 images). **Photolibrary:** Jupiterimages / Pixland (cla). **Science Photo Library:** Sheila Terry (tr). **68 Corbis:** Bettmann (main image); Dean Conger (bl). **69 Corbis:** Dave G. Houser (bl); image100 (crb/logs); Johannes Mann (tr); Skyscan (cr). **Getty Images:** Gregg Brown (crb/landfill); ChinaFotoPress (tl); Laurence Monneret / Photographer's Choice (br/giraffe). **iStockphoto.com:** Alija (cra). **70 Corbis:** Daniel Attia (crb); Rob Chatterson (cl). **Getty Images:** Raul Garcia / Flickr (bl); Sylvain Sonnet / Photographer's Choice (cra). **71 Corbis:** Jon Arnold / JAI (clb). **Getty Images:** Alessandra Benedetti / Bloomberg (cra); Patrick Hertzog / AFP (cb). **Photolibrary:** Adina Tovy / Robert Harding Travel (br). **72 Corbis:** Bettmann (tl). **72-73 Corbis:** Bohemian Nomad Picturemakers (bc/street scene); Holger Spiering / Westend61 (t/hilly landscape). **73 Alamy Images:** Andrew Holt (crb). **Lonely Planet Images:** Christopher Groenhout (tr). **74 Alamy Images:** Paul Glendell (cra). **Corbis:** Mike Theiss / Ultimate Chase (main image); Bernd Vogel (tr). **75 Corbis:** Jorge Ferrari / EPA (b); Radius Images (tl); Phil Schermeister (bl); Richard Schultz (cra). **76 Corbis:** Bertrand Gardel / Hemis (bc/car); John Harper (t); Christian Kober / JAI (cla). **iStockphoto.com:** Alija (bl). **77 Alamy Images:** Penny Tweedie (cb). **Corbis:** Construction Photography (bl); Envision (cr/groceries); Rick Gomez (cla); Michael Hanson (cra/class); Russ Heinl / All Canada Photos (cl/city); Nick Rochowski / View (ca); Tomas Rodriguez (cra/diving). **Getty Images:** Robin MacDougall (br). **78 Alamy Images:** David Cunningham (cla). **Getty Images:** K. Asif / India Today Group (tr); Chad Ehlers (br); Stephen Schauer (bl). **78-79 Getty Images:** Kim Jae-Myoung / AFP (roads with traffic). **79 Alamy Images:** Thomas Kraft / Transtock Inc. (br). **Getty Images:** Mark Horn / The Image Bank (cra/cockpit); Image Source (crb); Imagewerks Japan (tc). **80 Corbis:** Destinations (cra/pyramids); Kevin R. Morris (cr). **Getty Images:** Marco Cristofori / Robert Harding World Imagery (cra/Stonehenge); Gavin Hellier / Robert Harding World Imagery (cra/Colosseum); Davis McCardle / The Image Bank (cl); David Sanger / The Image Bank (cra/Taj Mahal). **80-81 Photolibrary:** Murat Ayranci / Superstock (b). **81 Alamy Images:** Deborah Thompson (cra). **Corbis:** Scott Andrews / Science Faction (ftl); Bettmann (tl). **Getty Images:** Visions of Our Land / The Image Bank (cl). **Photolibrary:** Brent Winebrenner (cr). **82 Corbis:** Pablo Otin / EPA (cra); Skyscan (cl). **82-83 Getty Images:** Peter Adams (b). **83 Alamy Images:** Cairney Down (ca/sign). **Getty Images:** Digitaler Lumpensammler / Flickr (tl); Tim Hall (cr). **84 Corbis:** Lester Lefkowitz (tl). **84-85 Alamy Images:** Janine Wiedel Photolibrary (c/crowd). **85 Corbis:** Bryan Reynolds / Science Faction (cra). **Getty Images:** AFP (tl). **88 Alamy Images:** Arctic Images (br); Norma Jean Gargasz (bl). **Corbis:** Ocean (cr). **Getty Images:** Stefano Oppo (cl); Photo 24 (bc); Hein von Horsten (c). **89 Corbis:** Dave Reede / All Canada Photos (main image). **90 Corbis:** Jane Sweeney / JAI (fbr). **Getty Images:** Diego Giudice / Bloomberg (harvest). **91 Corbis:** Marnie Burkhart / Fancy (bl/gas burner); Image Source (ftl); George Steinmetz (ftr). **Getty Images:** Per-Anders Pettersson / Reportage (bl/diamonds); Tim Graham (br); Rizwan Tabassum / AFP (cra/stockbroker). **92 Alamy Images:** sciencephotos (crb/coal). **Corbis:** Dr. James Richardson / Visuals Unlimited (crb/trunk). **Getty Images:** Richard Drury / Digital Vision (cr/bricks); Paul McCormick (cra/sheep). **92-93 Getty Images:** Yawar Kabli / Barcroft India (bl/woman); Yawar Nazir (workers in field). **93 Alamy Images:** Will Stanton (cb/books); Jack Sullivan (cb/Monopoly house). **Corbis:** Sagel & Kranefeld (c/coins). **Getty Images:** Thomas Barwick (ca); Cathy Crawford (cl/textile); Spencer Jones / FoodPix (clb/household goods); Siegfried Layda / Photographer's Choice (br); Balint Porneczi / AFP (tr); Monty Rakusen / Cultura (cla/steel workers); Dieter Spears / iStock Exclusive (clb/pump). **94 Corbis:** Peter Adams (cla); Jean-Pierre Amet (clb); Brooks Kraft (cl). **NASA:** Dr Heinz Linke (r). **95 Corbis:** Andy Aitchison (br); Guido Cozz / Atlantide Phototravel (ca); James Leynse (cra). **96 Getty Images:** Gregg Brown (main image) **97 Alamy Images:** Francis Vachon (cra). **FLPA:** Flip Nicklin / Minden Pictures (bl). **Getty Images:** Toledano (ca); Dougal Waters / Digital Vision (cla). **OceanwideImages.com:** Gary Bell (clb). **Science Photo Library:** Planetary Visions Ltd (br). **98 Corbis:** Frank Lukasseck (t). **Getty Images:** Howard Grey (bl); Keiji Iwai (ca/people). **iStockphoto.com:** Andriy Bezuglov (crb); Victor Maffe (cra/balloon). **99 Getty Images:** Max Dannenbaum (cr/astronaut); Laurence Monneret (br/safari); Paul Mansfield Photography / Flickr (clb); Will Sanders (ca). **iStockphoto.com:** luminis (ftl); narvikk (tr). **100 Corbis:** So Hing-Keung (cla); Munish Sharma / Reuters (bl); Tetra Images (br). **Getty Images:** Ira Block / National Geographic (tr). **101 Corbis:** So Hing-Keung (bl). **Getty Images:** Foodcollection (br); Trupti Patkar / Barcroft Media (tc); Manan Vatsyayana / AFP (tl). **Photolibrary:** Robert Dowey / Real Latino Images (cb). **102 Dorling Kindersley:** National Maritime Museum, London (tr). **103 Alamy Images:** The Art Gallery Collection (tr); Ilene MacDonald (cla); John Robertson (cra). **Getty Images:** Ghislain & Marie David deLossy (crb/tourists); Shannon Fagan (tl); Nacivet (crb/forest). **Science Photo Library:** Pasquale Sorrentino (cr). **104 Alamy Images:** The Art Gallery Collection (cb). **Ancient Art & Architecture Collection:** (tr); Interfoto (br). **Corbis:** Bettmann (cla). **De Agostini Editore:** (bl). **105 Ancient Art & Architecture Collection:** (tr). **Corbis:** Bettmann (ftl). **Fredrikson Map Collection, University of Jyvaskyla, Department of History and Ethnology/Eero and Erkki Fredrikson Foundation:** (crb). **Science Photo Library:** Sheila Terry (bl). **106 Corbis:** Yann Arthus-Bertrand (cla/Arc de Triomphe). **107 Getty Images:** Peter Cade (tr). **108 Flickr.com:** Rituparna Choudhury (br). **Planetary Visions Limited:** (cra). **109 Dorling Kindersley:** Natural History Museum, London (b/butterflies). **Getty Images:** Anna Henly (br); Nacivet (bc). **110 NASA:** Goddard Space Flight Center Scientific Visualization Studio (cra/globes x). **Wikipedia, The Free Encyclopedia:** NASA Goddard Space Flight Center (br). **111 © 1979, Stuart McArthur, www.ODTmaps.com:** McArthur's Universal Corrective Map of the World (b). **Planetary Visions Limited:** (t/map). **Wikipedia, The Free Encyclopedia:** NASA Goddard Space Flight Center (bl). **112 Science Photo Library:** David Ducros (b); Pasquale Sorrentino (tr). **113 Alamy Images:** John Robertson (tl). **National Geophysical Data Centre:** NGDC / NOAA (br). **Science Photo Library:** NASA (crb) (clb). **114 Alamy Images:** Rob Wilkinson (tr). **Getty Images:** Ghislain & Marie David deLossy (br). **iStockphoto.com:** Richard Simpkins (cl). **115 Alamy Images:** Alex Segre (br). **Getty Images:** AFP (bl). **iStockphoto.com:** Jan Rysavy (tr). **117 Science Photo Library:** Planetobserver (bc); © 1995, Worldsat International & J. Knighton (br/interrupted world map projection). **118 Corbis:** James Marshall (br). **Getty Images:** altrendo images (tr); Paul Chesley (cla); Medioimages / Photodisc (bl). **119 Corbis:** Stefano Amantini / Atlantide Phototravel (cra); Frans Lanting (tr). **Getty Images:** Bavaria (br); Frans Lemmens / Photographer's Choice (bl); Robin Smith (cla). **120 Corbis:** Amyn Nasser (bl). **122-123 Getty Images:** Nat Photos (b). **124-125 Alamy Images:** Richard Green / Commercial (b).

All other images © Dorling Kindersley
For further information see: www.dkimages.com

Acknowledgements

Dorling Kindersley would also like to thank: Peter Bull and Simon Mumford for artworks; Rachael Grady, Poppy Joslin, Pamela Shiels, and Sadie Thomas for design assistance; Myriam Mégharbi for help with picture research; Holly Beaumont, Deborah Lock, Lorrie Mack, and Fleur Star for editorial assistance.